Bricklaying and Stone Masonry

by Richard T. Kreh, Sr.

Drawings by Mel Erikson

POPULAR SCIENCE BOOKS

Published by

Popular Science Books
Times Mirror Magazines, Inc.
380 Madison Avenue
New York, NY 10017

Library of Congress Catalog Card Number: 80-5208
ISBN: 0-06-090876-9

Manufactured in the United States of America

Contents

Preface

This is a book for the home handyman who wants to improve his grounds with masonry projects.

The projects described and illustrated in this book are just a sampling of what can be done with bricks, stone, and mortar. The possibilities are virtually limitless. And, owing to the durability of the materials, the life-span of a properly built masonry project is incredibly long.

In these times of high prices and runaway inflation, it's a great advantage to be able to do your own masonry work. It's extremely difficult to get a professional mason to do a small job, as the margin of profit is so low; and if he does agree to do it, you often are overcharged. But just as important as the money saved are the satisfaction and sense of achievement that come from doing a masonry job yourself. Bricklaying and stonework are creative, relaxing pastimes, especially if you work behind a desk all day.

I would like to thank my wife, who typed the manuscript; my son Ricky and my brother Lefty for their assistance in taking photos. Thanks are also due to the Brick Institute of America and the National Lime Association for their technical help, as well as to the many friends who took the time to discuss their masonry projects with me.

So . . . clean off your mortar boards and let's go to work . . .

RICHARD T. KREH, SR.
Frederick, Maryland

1 | Bricks and Mortar

Bricks have been used as a building material for centuries. The earliest form was the adobe brick, which was made by pressing clay into a block and allowing it to dry and harden in the sun. Excavations in the Tigres-Euphrates basin have uncovered adobe bricks over 5,000 years old. The Babylonians, Persians, and Assyrians all used bricks for building walls and other structures.

Eventually, it was learned that burning clay blocks in a kiln hardened them and made them fireproof. The Romans manufactured such burned bricks in large quantities and used them in building throughout the empire, generally concealing them behind a facade of stone or marble. The Byzantines, however, allowed the brick to show, setting a trend that culminated in the Middle Ages in the decorative brickwork of Italy and Germany. During the Renaissance, brick architecture was developed to a high degree of sophistication in England.

Handmade bricks were produced in the American colonies as early as 1611. With the invention of the steam engine, power-driven machines replaced manual labor in brick manufacture. The first brick-making machine was patented in 1800.

Today, bricks are manufactured of clay and shale, both of which are found in the earth in their natural state. Shale, which is actually clay that has been compressed into layers in the ground, is a dense material and more difficult to extract; hence it is more costly. Clay and shale are mixed in certain proportions to achieve the proper consistency, formed into blocks and fired in a kiln at a high and uniform temperature. In the early days of brickmaking, it was not always possible to subject bricks in a kiln to uniform heat. As a result, bricks fired in the same batch had different characteristics and were given different names—clinker, red, soft, salmon, rough hard, straight hard, and bloat. The term "clinker," which refers to an overburned, twisted brick, has come to mean any bad item in a batch. The Federal Trade Commission has ruled that only products made from clay and shale, and burned in a kiln, can be called *brick.* Otherwise, the name must include the material from which the brick is made—cinder brick, concrete brick, etc.

Two general categories of bricks are available: building (or common) bricks and face bricks. Common bricks are made as just described but, as they do not have to meet special standards of color, texture, or design, they are less expensive than face bricks. They are generally used as filler bricks or backing material, unless their rough texture and varying colors are needed to create a rustic appearance. Face bricks, as the name implies, are used on the front of a wall. They are manufactured under controlled conditions and must meet specifications established by the American Society for Testing Materials.

BUYING BRICK. Check your area for a building-supply dealer that specializes in brick and caters to professional masons or contractors. His

The five most popular sizes of brick available at building-supply dealers. Of them all, the standard brick is most often used.

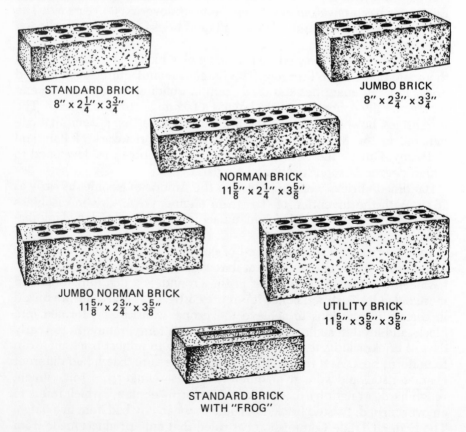

STANDARD BRICK
$8'' \times 2\frac{1}{4}'' \times 3\frac{3}{4}''$

JUMBO BRICK
$8'' \times 2\frac{3}{4}'' \times 3\frac{3}{4}''$

NORMAN BRICK
$11\frac{5}{8}'' \times 2\frac{1}{4}'' \times 3\frac{5}{8}''$

JUMBO NORMAN BRICK
$11\frac{5}{8}'' \times 2\frac{3}{4}'' \times 3\frac{5}{8}''$

UTILITY BRICK
$11\frac{5}{8}'' \times 3\frac{5}{8}'' \times 3\frac{5}{8}''$

STANDARD BRICK
WITH "FROG"

prices will usually be lower than the home center that carries a lot of other materials and brick as a sideline. When you visit the dealer, don't be confused by the many types and colors of bricks on display. You will probably select one of the five types shown in the accompanying photo. Most often used is the so-called standard brick, which measures approximately 8" by 2¼" by 3¾" and weighs around 4 to 4½ pounds. Throughout this book, references to brick will be to this standard size unless otherwise stated. At most dealers, different bricks of varying textures and colors are displayed in sample panels or bundles. The bricks are arranged in a half-over pattern with mortar joints between them. This is done by gluing sample bricks to a hardboard backing with simulated mortar joints, to show how different bricks will look in a wall. A manufacturer's order number will be on the sample; check to be sure the correct number is on your order. Bricks are also displayed in stacks held by metal carrying bands. These are handy for brick salesmen to show a customer at home or on the job.

Samples of bricks displayed in a dealer's showroom. Each sample is assigned a manufacturer's number, which is used when ordering.

A variety of bricks of different colors and finishes bound with metal carrying bands. Sheets of hardboard between bricks simulate mortar joints, permit you to see different color combinations of bricks and mortar.

Bricks can be obtained in different textures or finishes—for example, sandy-speckled face, matt or scored irregular face, Colonial sand, and semismooth face. The treatment of the mortar joints after the bricks have been laid also will enhance the texture. Hand-molded bricks are available to lend an old-fashioned appearance to a wall.

Bricks may be solid, or have vertical holes in the interior, or an indented area in the bottom. The holes and indentation allow the mortar to lock the

Bricks are available with various textures. At left, a reproduction of an old-fashioned sand-speckled finish; center, a scored finish; at right, a Colonial sand finish.

A hand-molded, sand-face brick used in Colonial reproductions.

Two types of cored bricks and one with an indented "frog." Both the cores and the "frog" help the mortar joint to lock the brick securely in place.

A banded cube of 500 bricks. The cube weighs slightly over a ton. Banding protects the bricks from chipping during shipment.

brick securely in the joint. The indentation is known as a "frog" and should always be on the underside when the brick is laid in the mortar bed. Solid bricks are usually selected for walks, patios, and other projects where holes would be unsightly. When buying bricks, examine the color and finish, and check to see if they are fairly hard and straight, and all close to the same size. You can test bricks at the supplier by striking them together. If they have been burned properly, they should emit a metallic ringing sound.

Be careful of old used or reclaimed bricks. To determine if reclaimed bricks are hard enough, you can perform the strike test. If the bricks make a dull, thudding sound, they are too soft to use in an exterior wall or project. Also, discard bricks that are a light pinkish color, with pieces of white flint on the surface; they are too soft.

Bricks are sold singly or by the thousand lot. If you are buying a truck-load, naturally they will be less expensive. Due to the rising cost of fuel, the price of bricks has increased dramatically in recent years. For this reason, any prices quoted as this book goes to press will soon be out of date. There is a substantial delivery cost, so if you have an old pickup truck or trailer, it will be worth your time to pick up the bricks yourself.

If you buy bricks in cubes of 500, they will be held together with metal bands to make transporting them easier and to reduce chipping. Be careful when hauling loose bricks not to damage their edges. This can be avoided by stacking them on cardboard or putting straw in between the rows.

It may be well to remember that an average cube of 500 bricks will weigh in excess of one ton (2,000 pounds), far too much weight to haul in a half-ton pickup truck. Make two or more trips.

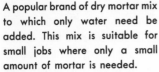

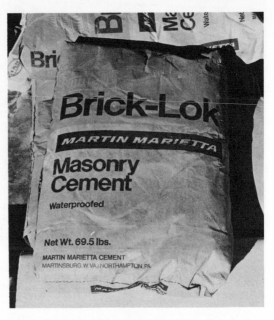

A popular brand of dry mortar mix to which only water need be added. This mix is suitable for small jobs where only a small amount of mortar is needed.

Masonry-cement mix is combined with sand and water to make mortar. This mix is more economical to use for large jobs which require a lot of mortar.

MORTAR FOR BRICKLAYING. You will need materials for mixing mortar before you can lay any brick. For a small job, buy a dry-mix mortar that only requires the addition of water. For larger jobs, it is more economical to buy masonry cement to which you add sand and water in the proper proportions. Or, you can buy portland cement and hydrated lime and make high-strength mortar by adding sand and water. As portland cement-lime mortar is a bit more work to mix, it is seldom used by the home handyman except for special jobs such as stonework.

The following mortar mixes are recommended for average brickwork.

Dry-mix prepackaged mortar. Add enough water to the mix to make mortar of the proper stiffness for the job at hand. A good rule to follow is not to mix more mortar than you can use in one hour. If all the mortar has been used and it is close to lunch time, quit a bit early rather than make up another batch and have it set during the lunch break. Mortar can be tempered (adding water that is lost due to evaporation) once or twice if it starts to set up in the pan, but be careful of adding more than that as it will seriously weaken the mixture. Don't use old mortar that has a lot of hard lumps in it; it will not only be difficult to work, but will be weak due to hydration. Throw it away and get some new cement. However, as long as you keep a mortar mix in a dry place, tightly sealed and off a damp floor, it will remain usable indefinitely.

Bags of portland cement and hydrated lime for making portland cement-lime mortar. By combining these materials in different proportions, you can vary the strength of mortar.

Dry-mix concrete, like its mortar counterpart, requires only the addition of water. Again, this is suitable for small jobs.

Masonry cement. The general-purpose formula is 1 part masonry cement to 3 parts sand. If you want to mix half a bag, add nine dirt shovels of sand. Adding eighteen shovels of sand to a whole bag will make up what is called a full batch, but be sure you can use this much without it setting up too fast.

Portland cement-lime mortar. For normal mortar mixes, buy Type 1 portland cement. Mix one part (or one shovel) portland cement to one part (or one shovel) hydrated lime to six parts (or six shovels) sand. This is known as an average strength, Type N mortar. It will make a strong mortar with approximately 750 pounds compressive strength to the square inch. This will surpass almost any strength requirements you will need for repair or home construction. Mixes stronger than this for portland cement-lime mortars are known as design mixes, which you need not be concerned about.

SAND. The importance of using good sand in mixing mortar cannot be overemphasized. Sand for mortar should be free of silt or dirt. When silt is present, it does not allow the cement in the mix to surround the sand particles; the result is a weak mortar. Dirty sand will produce a sticky or gummy mortar that clings to the trowel. Cheap siltsand which has not been washed commercially is no bargain and will cause great difficulty.

Testing for clean sand. Handful at left, when squeezed into a ball, remains compressed, indicating presence of dirt or silt. Handful at right remains loose after squeezing, indicating clean sand.

Here is a simple test you can make on the spot to determine if sand is relatively clean: Pick up a handful and squeeze it into a ball. If the sand remains in a ball when you open your hand, it contains too much dirt. This test cannot be made with wet sand.

ESTIMATING MATERIALS. Rule-of-thumb estimating is the simplest method of figuring how much masonry materials you need. This system was developed by masons over the years through trial and error and is accurate for jobs up to house size. For large commercial jobs, an estimator or masonry contractor would use special tables. However, you can use the figures given here with confidence. They include a reasonable amount for waste.

When estimating a job at home, don't buy more than you need; you can always obtain extra materials. If you have too much material left over, it will probably sit around for a long time before you get a chance to use it. Your supplier may allow unused materials to be returned. Some suppliers deduct 10 percent from the refund. Nevertheless, expect to have a little material left over as it is impossible to estimate how many bricks may be chipped or cracked or *exactly* how much mortar or sand will be needed.

How many bricks? To estimate the number of standard bricks, you must first determine the amount of square footage in the wall or project. If the total does not come out evenly, round off to the next highest number; it is always better to have a little extra than to be short. If there are any openings in the wall, deduct them in square feet.

Mortar joints are always included in the square footage, so you need not allow extra for them. As a rule, the mortar head and bed joints will be either ⅜″ or ½″ in thickness for regular brick. Old, used bricks will probably take ½″ due to irregularities in size.

Let's say you want to build a wall 2′ high and 30′ long. First, determine the area of the wall (2 × 30 = 60 square feet). To find out how many bricks are needed, multiply 60 by 7 (there are about 7 bricks in every square foot of a wall). This will allow a small amount of waste, as, technically speaking, there are exactly 6.75 bricks in a square foot of wall including the mortar joints. The result is 420 bricks. But this wall will be built of two thicknesses of bricks. Therefore, double the figure 420 for a grand total of 840 bricks.

How much cement? Regardless of brand, masonry cement comes in 70-pound bags. To determine how much is needed, figure that one bag of masonry cement will lay 125 bricks. Now, divide 125 into 840 bricks. The answer is 6.72 bags. Since you can't buy part of a bag, you will need 7 bags of masonry cement to do the job.

If you're using dry-mix: Each bag will lay approximately 50 bricks. The only thing you add to this mix is water.

If you're using portland cement-lime mortar: For an average strength mortar (Type N), 1 bag of portland cement and 1 bag of hydrated lime with 42 shovels of sand will lay approximately 300 bricks. This is what is considered a full batch. Smaller batches can be made of course by mixing 1 part portland cement to 1 part lime to 6 parts sand.

Estimating mortar for laying concrete blocks is done as follows:

1 bag of masonry cement to 17 shovels of sand (sand measured with a standard dirt shovel) will lay approximately 25 concrete blocks. If you're laying 4″ × 8″ × 16″ blocks, you could increase this to 30 blocks.

1 bag of prepackaged dry-mix mortar will lay approximately 17 blocks.

1 bag of portland cement to 1 bag of hydrated lime to 42 shovels of sand will lay approximately 62 concrete blocks. All of these mixes could vary a little depending on job conditions but are good averages.

How much sand? This is the most inexpensive of all masonry materials. To estimate sand, figure that 1 ton will make enough mortar to lay 1,000 bricks. For small jobs, remember that you mix 9 shovels of sand to half a bag of masonry cement, or a ratio of 1 to 3. To mix a full bag use 18 shovels of sand. This is known in the trade as one batch. For smaller amounts of sand, estimate how many bricks you are going to lay and adjust the amount of sand to this number.

When doing a small job, if a pickup truck is not available take some burlap bags to the building-supply dealer and have him fill them with sand. Some dealers even supply the bags. A burlap bag holds about 100 pounds of sand. Dump the leftovers in the kids' sandbox when the job is finished.

An important point to remember about buying sand: if at least a half ton is needed, be sure to place it on a hard surface and not on the ground. Sand has a way of disappearing into the ground in a hurry. Also, it is a good idea in cold weather to cover the sand so the water in it doesn't freeze.

METAL REINFORCEMENT. There are times when you will need some type of metal wall tie or joint reinforcement. Some of the most often used ones are shown on the next page. The corrugated veneer tie is made

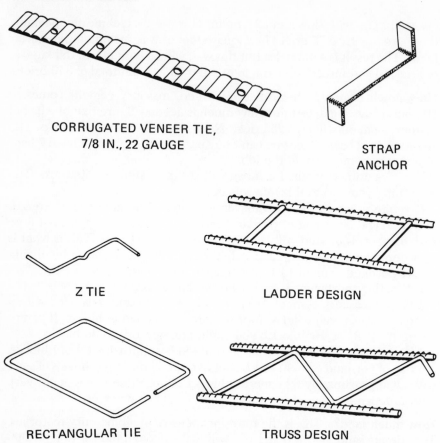

CORRUGATED VENEER TIE,
7/8 IN., 22 GAUGE

STRAP
ANCHOR

Z TIE

LADDER DESIGN

RECTANGULAR TIE

TRUSS DESIGN

Metal reinforcements used in bricklaying and stonework.

of galvanized metal. It is approximately 8″ long and ⅞″ wide. It contains a number of holes so it can be nailed to wood framing, bent down onto the brick, and walled into the mortar joint. It is used to bond brick veneer to house framing.

Z-ties are made of heavy metal wire and are used in bonding a cavity wall. A cavity wall has an air space in the middle for insulation; the tie has a crimp in its center to allow moisture that builds up in the wall to drip off. Weep holes at the bottom of the wall allow water to seep out. The rectangular steel tie can be used in place of the Z-tie. It is available with or without a crimp in the center.

When bonding a masonry main wall to a partition wall, the flat steel strap anchor can be used.

Steel joint reinforcement is used to strengthen masonry walls or to bond

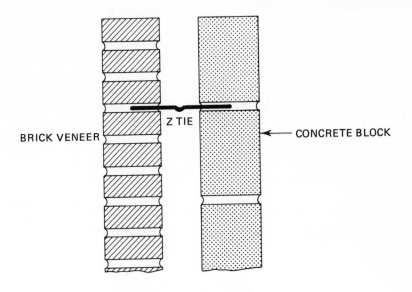

Z-tie bonds brick veneer to concrete-block wall.

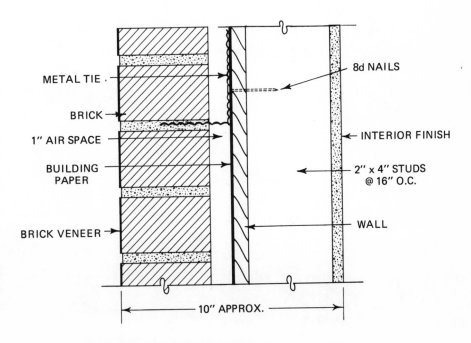

Corrugated veneer tie bonds brick veneer to house framing.

two different types of masonry materials, such as brick and concrete block. Two basic types are the truss and the ladder. The truss design is the most popular.

Metal ties should be installed every 16″ in height and no more than 36″ inches apart. Make sure the tie is fully imbedded in the mortar joint. Steel joint reinforcement should be overlapped at least 8″.

All of the metal ties described are available at building-supply dealers. The corrugated veneer ties can be purchased singly or in cartons of 1,000. Z-ties, rectangular ties, and strap anchors are sold singly. Steel joint rein-

Steel joint reinforcement is used to bond brickwork to concrete block (top) or to reinforce a block wall (bottom).

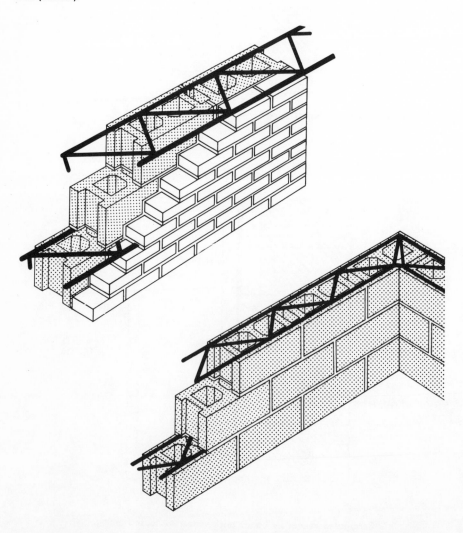

forcement is sold either by the bundle or in 10′ lengths. It is also available in different widths to suit various wall thicknesses.

Building-supply dealers also stock steel rods of different diameters for reinforcing concrete footings, walks, and floors.

2 | Tools and Equipment

The tools you need to do your own masonry work are neither numerous nor expensive. They can be bought at most good hardware or building-supply dealers. It is always a good idea to buy brand-name tools as they will pay off in the long run in longer wear. If a tool is defective, the dealer will, as a rule, make an adjustment, but beware of imported "bargain" tools found in many supermarkets and department stores. They are usually held together by simple spot welds or rivets and will fall apart with a little hard use. A quality tool has a good feel, when held in the hand, that you will come to appreciate as the job progresses. Remember: You only get what you pay for; select good tools at the outset.

Brick trowel. Let's start by selecting the basic masonry tool in your kit, the brick trowel. Most masons prefer the diamond-pattern heel trowel. I like the London pattern, and it can be obtained with either a narrow or wide heel. Although brick trowels are available in different lengths, you would be best served by buying a trowel no longer than 10½". The length is marked on the handle. For laying bricks, I prefer a narrow heel. If you are going to do a lot of block work, select one with a wide heel, to spread more mortar on the wall. Smaller trowels are available for pointing or patching work.

When you examine a trowel at the store, try these simple tests to determine if it is a good one. Strike the blade gently against a hard surface. It should emit a metallic ring, indicating that it was tempered correctly. Flex the blade against a flat surface. A good brick trowel should not be too stiff so it can flex when used to furrow mortar joints. The blade should bend easily and come back to its original shape. Check the balance of the trowel by allowing it to hang downward on your right index finger at the point where the shank meets the handle. It should balance easily and quickly. A trowel is held correctly with the thumb even with or slightly touching the front edge of the handle where it meets the shank.

Regular brick trowel with London pattern and smaller pointing trowel used for patching or pointing brickwork.

Checking the balance of a trowel. When suspended from index finger, trowel should hang straight.

Checking the flex of a trowel. When the point is pushed against a hard surface, trowel should flex and then return to its original shape when pressure is released.

Proper way to hold a trowel. Thumb rests on the front edge of the handle; the grip is firm but the hand is relaxed.

Standard brick hammer with wood handle.

Brick hammer. This tool is used for cutting brick and other masonry materials. It has a square head on one side and a chisel on the other. A good blade is tempered to the correct hardness for cutting masonry materials. Once it is dulled, try to find a local blacksmith who will heat and hammer the cutting edge and retemper it to the proper hardness. Merely grinding the edge on a wheel will take the temper out of the steel quickly and cause it to break. I recommend buying a 16- or 18-ounce hammer for general work. The handle choice is up to you, but my preference is wood.

Levels. The traditional bricklayer's level (also called a plumb rule) is 48 inches long. Shorter ones, 24 or 18 inches long, are available for tight places. I prefer a wood level as the mortar will not stick to it as easily. I also suggest that you buy a level with vials filled with alcohol rather than

Levels used for bricklaying. Long one measures 48", short one 24".

Apply linseed oil to level with soft cloth to preserve wood. Don't smear the oil on glass area or it will obscure bubbles in vial.

oil. In extremely hot or cold weather an oil bubble will expand or shrink, whereas an alcohol bubble does not change. The level is a delicate tool, so treat it gently.

When the bubble in the level is between the marked lines, it is said to be "true." Holding the level against the work in a vertical position is known as "plumbing" the work. Holding the level horizontally is known as "leveling" the work.

To prolong the life of a wooden level, rub it with linseed oil after use.

Line blocks and pins. In the course of building a brick wall, it will be necessary to attach a line from one corner to another. This line is used as a guide to lay the bricks in the wall. Lines can be attached to a brick wall with a steel pin on one end and a nail on the other end, or with a factory-made set of line blocks. Line blocks and pins can be obtained at most building-supply dealers. Also, a metal trig is used on a long wall to stop the line from sagging. Its use will be explained later in the chapter on laying brick.

Chisels. These come in a number of sizes and shapes. The ones you'll need for regular masonry work are the brick-set chisel, which is used for

Tools used for attaching a line to a brick wall: pair of line blocks, line pin, common nail, trig.

Three chisels used in bricklaying; (from left): wide brick set, standard all-purpose chisel, plugging or joint chisel.

cutting brick pieces to size; the standard chisel, which is used for cutting out old work; and the plugging, or joint, chisel, which has a tapered blade that is used to remove old mortar joints.

Steel square.   Needed for squaring the corners of the walls and openings. Get a carpenter's 2' framing square. It will handle all your squaring jobs.

Jointing tool.   Once the bricks have been laid in the wall and the mortar joints are firm, a striking or jointing tool is used to seal and add special effects to the mortar. These come in a variety of styles and sizes. If a half-round indentation is desired (concave joint) the convex striking tool is used. This is the tool I would recommend as your best choice for an all-around finish. Buy a large one, say ⅝″ on one end and ¾″ on the opposite end. The larger size will fill out the mortar joint evenly without pressing it in too much.

There are other striking tools you can use for forming various types of mortar joints. The V-jointer is a small piece of angle iron mounted on a wood handle which leaves a V-shaped impression in the mortar joint. The grapevine jointer tool has a raised bead of steel on it; when drawn through the mortar joint, it leaves a thin line in the joint. It is a favorite for tooling colonial reproductions. A flat piece of steel is used for flush joints, such as those in pavings or steps, and is called a slicker striking tool. Last, the rake-out jointing tool is used for gouging mortar joints to a predetermined depth. The best one on the market is mounted on two small wheels with a thumbscrew in the center which permits adjusting the nail to the desired depth. You rarely should rake a joint deeper than ⅜″ or it may leak.

Jointers used for bricklaying (from top): V-shaped sled runner, convex sled runner, convex jointer.

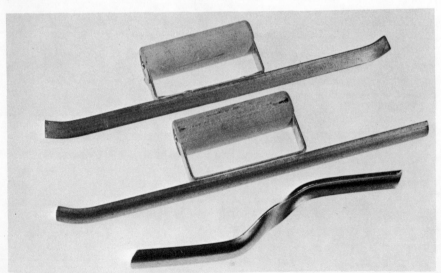

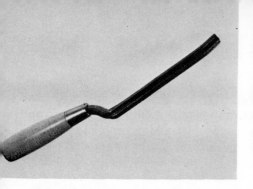

Grapevine jointer has a raised bead of steel which leaves an indentation in the center of the joint.

Flat steel jointer, called a slicker, is used to form flush, smooth joints in brick walls.

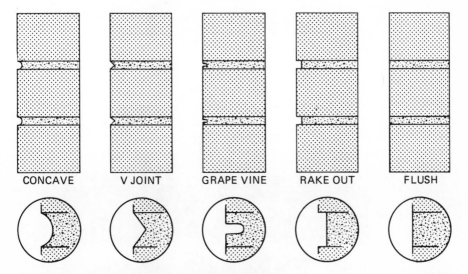

Rake-out jointer is used for gouging mortar joints. Nail can be set for varying depths.

Profiles of five popular mortar joints.

CONCAVE   V JOINT   GRAPE VINE   RAKE OUT   FLUSH

Pocket rule. Needed to measure and lay out the job. There are two different types of rules used for masonry work, the modular rule (based on the 4″ module or grid) and the course counter rule. Most probably you will not need both types, so I would buy the modular rule.

Another handy tool to have is a steel tapemeasure. The most practical size is 50′ to 100′.

Mason's line. Buy one of nylon, size No. 18, 250′. The twisted line is less expensive than the braided and will work just as well. Lines are sold in colors and on binders or in balls.

Chalk box and brush. These are necessities for bricklaying. An old stove brush has long been a favorite of masons.

Complete your set of tools with something to carry them around in—a clean 5-gallon pail, or an old gym bag.

Two types of folding mason's rules. Top one is spacing rule, also called a course counter; bottom one is modular spacing rule.

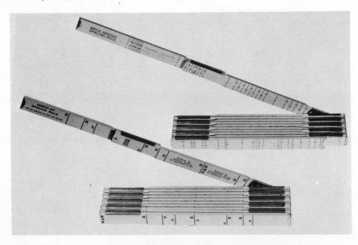

100-foot steel tape.

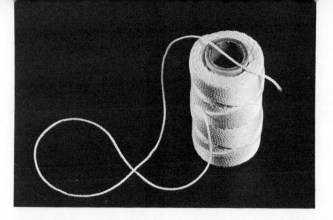

Nylon line used for masonry work. End should be sealed with a match to prevent unraveling.

Chalk box and stove-type brush.

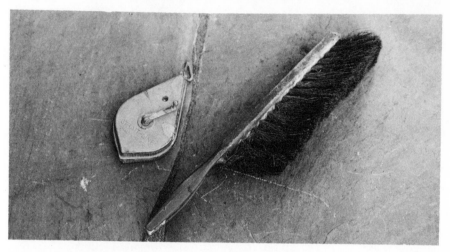

Tool display board at building-supply dealer.

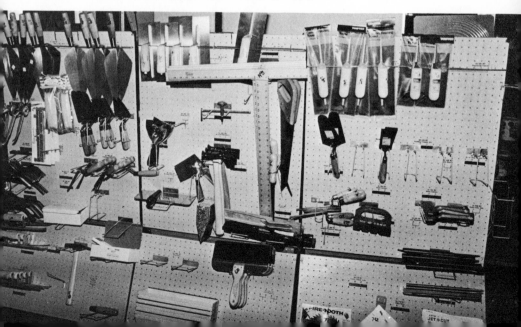

Contractor's wheelbarrow is used for mixing or transporting mortar and masonry materials.

Wheelbarrow. If mortar is to be mixed in a wheelbarrow, select one with rubber tires and a capacity of 5 cubic feet.

Mortar box. If a wheelbarrow is not used for mixing mortar, then you will need a mortar mixing box. There are, of course, factory-made metal mixing boxes available from your building-supply dealer, but you can construct one easily from scrap boards. A good size for small jobs is 24″ by 60″ by 12″. Make the ends on a slant for easier mixing and removal of mortar.

Mortar hoe. To mix mortar, you will need a mortar hoe that has two holes in the center, and a standard dirt shovel. A regular garden hoe can be used to mix mortar, but one with holes makes the work easier.

Mortar board. You will need some type of receptacle to place the mortar on after it has been mixed. A mortar board is the answer. Mortar is easily worked off the board with the trowel and onto the wall. A wooden mortar board 30″ square can be built of some scrap boards or plywood. There should be two wood runners—lengths of 2×4—to raise it off the ground.

Other equipment needed you will probably find around the house, such as a length of garden hose, a few buckets, and an old brush for cleanup.

Cement mixer. Mortar can be mixed more easily with a drum-type cement mixer, so if you have a large job to do, you might want to rent one. The price of these mixers has risen sharply in the last few years—along with everything else—but if you plan on doing a number of large jobs in the future, you may want to buy one. They currently cost between $300 and $400.

Dirt shovel and mortar hoe used for preparing mortar.

Utility mixer powered by gasoline engine can be used for mixing mortar or concrete for small jobs.

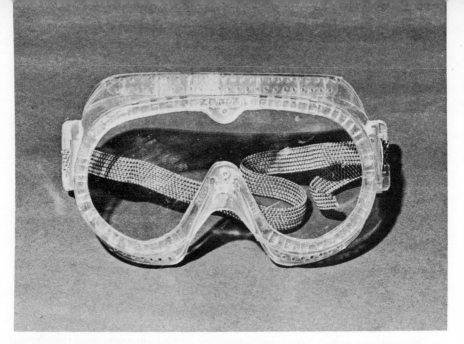

Safety goggles with soft plastic frame should be worn when cutting brick.

Goggles. Eye protection in the form of goggles or glasses is a must when cutting bricks or working around flying chips of any kind. Goggles are particularly valuable when cutting out old mortar joints or brick with a chisel.

Scaffolds. If your project requires the use of a scaffold, you can rent frames or you can improvise with sawhorses and scrap lumber. Be sure that the scaffold will hold all your materials plus your weight safely. The planks should be free of large knots or splits. Test the scaffold by jumping up and down on it before stocking materials. A claw hammer, handsaw, and crowbar are needed to build a scaffold.

Cleanup. It is especially important to clean masonry tools immediately after use, as mortar will stick and cause rust. Once a wheelbarrow's bed gets pitted with rust, the next mix will stick, making it very difficult to use. Brick trowels and other hand tools should always be cleaned and wiped with an old cloth before putting them away. Your tools and equipment will last a long time and be a pleasure to use if you take good care of them.

3 | Building a Foundation

Before starting any brick project, visit your local department of building permits and find out if you need a permit. As a rule, no permit is needed for such small projects as outdoor fireplaces, walks, or garden walls, but check anyway.

The department will also tell you how far the project must be set back from existing property lines. Reread your deed to see if there are any limitations or restrictions to building on your property.

Any sizable masonry project requires some kind of foundation. You cannot merely spread mortar on the ground and start to build a brick wall. You need a solid base on which to lay the bricks. The depth of the foundation is determined by the frost line in your area. For example, in the Middle Atlantic states in which I live, the frost line is approximately 18″ to 24″ deep, depending on the severity of the winter. In a state such as Florida, there may be no frost line at all, but you would still need a base on which to distribute the weight of the wall. When the ground freezes and thaws, the earth heaves upward, causing masonry, which cannot flex, to break or crack.

Typical building permit for a construction job. Building inspector makes comments on the permit that indicate he has inspected job.

LAYING OUT BUILDING LINES. Before you begin excavating, you must lay out the project with stakes and lines. This cannot be done by eye. You'll need some wood stakes (lengths of 2×4s sharpened on one end), about eight 1×6 boards approximately 6' long, a supply of 8D common nails, and a ball of nylon line. A regular hammer will suffice for driving the stakes, but a sledgehammer will speed the job.

First, determine the building line and drive two stakes to mark each end.

Next, place a level mark on each stake. It is important to start out with a level building line. A simple method of doing this if the line is short (say, under 10') is to hold the ends of a straight 2×4 against the stakes, place a level on top, and, when you have leveled the 2×4, mark the stakes. (You may need a helper to do this.)

If the building line is longer than your 2×4, you can make an accurate level out of a plastic, transparent garden hose. Fill the hose with water. Stretch it on the ground between the two stakes and turn up the ends.

Establishing level points on two stakes with the aid of a long 2×4. This will serve as the main building line.

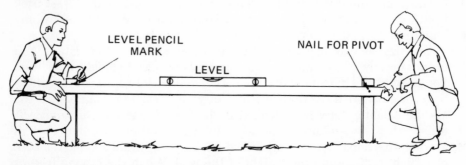

Length of garden hose can be used to establish level points. If hose is not transparent, short lengths of plastic tubing can be inserted in each end.

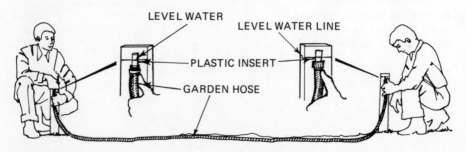

HOLDING GARDEN HOSE WITH
WATER IN FOR LEVEL LINE

Then mark the water level on the stakes. If your garden hose is not transparent, buy two 8″ lengths of plastic tubing which fit the inside diameter of the hose. You will be able to see the water level through the tubing.

Now you must lay out a square corner. If the project is less than 5′ long, you can hold a regular carpenter's framing square against the main line and stretch another line at right angles to it. If the project is longer than 5′, use the right triangle method. This is based on the theorem that the square of the hypotenuse of a right triangle is equal to the sum of the squares of the other two sides. Here one side is the main building line, the other side is the line you want to stretch at right angles to it, and the hypotenuse is the line that would connect them to form a right triangle. Thus if one side is 6′ and the other 8′ the sum of their squares (36 and 64) equals 100. The hypotenuse is therefore 10′ (10 × 10=100).

The theorem can be applied on a larger or smaller scale depending on the size of the project. The smallest scale generally used for squaring a corner of a small project is 3-4-5.

The 6-8-10 method of laying out a foundation is shown in the accompanying drawings. You need two assistants and two steel tapes.

To lay a building line at right angles to *A–B*, drive a stake at *C*, 8′ from stake *A*. Hammer nails into the tops of both stakes. Slip the end of one tape measure over the nail in stake *A*, and another tape measure over the nail in stake *C*. Bring the two tapes across each other so the 10′ mark on the tape attached to stake *C* hits the 6′ mark on the tape attached to stake *A*. Drive a stake at that point, *D*. The angle at stake *A* will be 90 degrees.

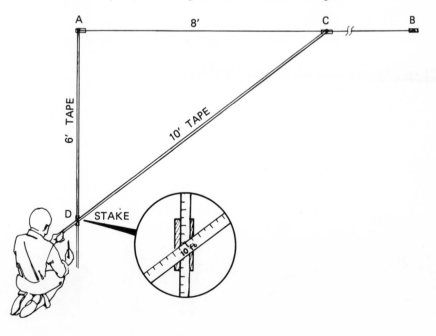

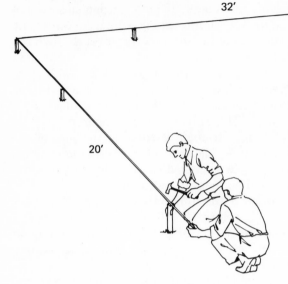

32'

20'

The next step is to extend the building line on the 6' leg of the triangle. If that side of the building is 20', stretch tape from stake *A* across the top of stake *D* and install stake *E* at the correct distance from stake *A*.

Once all building lines have been installed, check squareness with diagonal lines as shown below. If diagonals are equal in length, the rectangle is square.

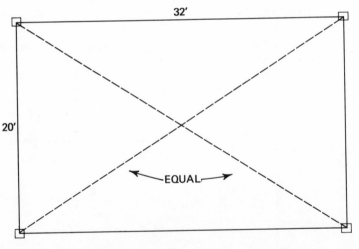

32'

20'

←EQUAL→

Transfer building lines to batter boards by lining them up with the stakes and marking the boards. Then drive nails into the edges of the boards and attach the lines.

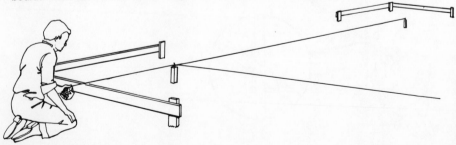

Once you have established two building lines with a square corner, it is only a matter of measuring the length and width of the project on these lines and driving stakes to mark the corners. You can then check the rectangle for square by measuring the diagonals. If square, they should be equal.

Batter boards. The next step is to transfer the building lines to wood corner guides called batter boards. Drive these 2×4 stakes about 4′ outside each corner stake to form a right angle. Then nail a 1×6 board to the stakes, making sure they are all level. Stretch lines from the stakes to the batter boards as shown in the diagrams below.

A completed layout for a foundation should have all building lines in place, with the batter boards set back 4′ from where the excavation will begin. This permits you to dig without disturbing the lines, which have to be maintained as reference points while the foundation is built.

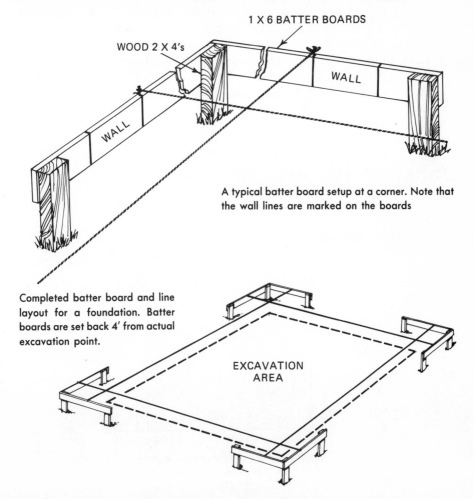

1 X 6 BATTER BOARDS

WOOD 2 X 4's

WALL

WALL

A typical batter board setup at a corner. Note that the wall lines are marked on the boards

Completed batter board and line layout for a foundation. Batter boards are set back 4′ from actual excavation point.

EXCAVATION AREA

POURING THE FOOTING. Your project may require a concrete footing on which to lay a concrete-block foundation. A trench must therefore be dug in which to pour the footing. A pick, mattock, digging iron, and shovel are needed to dig the trench. The rule for a concrete-block foundation wall is that the footing width should be twice the width of the concrete block it supports. For example, if an 8″ wide block is to be laid, then the footing should be 16″ wide. Footing depth is usually 8″, 12″, or 16″ for a fireplace or chimney. Check the building code in your area.

If the ground is inclined, a step footing can be installed to save concrete block. This is accomplished by digging steps and placing form boards in 8″ or 16″ divisions for the footing. The block wall is built in steps.

There are two basic types of concrete footings. If no rocks are found in the soil, the concrete can be poured in the bottom of the trench. If there are a lot of rocks in the soil, it is necessary to build wood forms to contain the concrete.

You can mix concrete by hand, use a utility mixer or, if a lot is needed, order from a transit-mix company. A good formula to follow when mixing your own concrete is 1 part portland cement to 2 parts sand to 3 parts crushed stone, with enough water to make it workable. Concrete delivered by transit truck comes on the job pre-mixed. A good mix to order for footings is known as a "five-bag mix." This means there are five bags of portland cement to each cubic yard of concrete. When the concrete is delivered, make sure you have left room to get the truck close to the trench.

Important: After concrete has been laid, immediately wash all tools. The concrete truck is equipped with a hose; ask the driver to spray your

An 8″ concrete block as it would appear centered on a 16″ footing.

FOOTING TWICE AS WIDE AS BLOCK
FOR GOOD WEIGHT DISTRIBUTION

Foundation trenches on a large housing project that have been excavated using batter boards and lines as a guide.

Concrete footing that has been poured in a trench to support a foundation wall. After the footing area was excavated, stakes were driven into the trench, leveled, and concrete poured to their tops.

tools before he leaves. Also, be careful where the truck washes excess concrete. Tell the driver to take any excess back to the plant and wash out the truck on the company's property.

Once the concrete is in place, let it dry for one day. Concrete takes about twenty-eight days to cure to full strength, but since it is supported by wood forms on the sides of the trench, there is no danger of damaging it. If the footing was poured into a form, leave it in place for at least two days.

LAYING THE BLOCK. For a small project, mortar can be mixed in a mud box or wheelbarrow.

To mix masonry-cement mortar, follow the steps shown in the accompanying photos.

MIXING MORTAR IN A WHEELBARROW

1. Put nine shovels of sand into the wheelbarrow (right).

2. Add half bag masonry cement. Mix well with shovel and hoe.

3. Pull the mix to one end of the wheelbarrow

4. Pour water into the empty end of the wheelbarrow.

5. Pull the dry mix into the water, working it until it is well mixed.

6. Test the mortar by picking up a trowel full and inverting the trowel. The mortar should cling. If the mortar does not cling to the trowel, add a little more masonry cement and mix well.

To establish the corners of the block foundation, reattach the lines to the batter boards and pull them tight. At each corner, drop a plumb bob from the point where the lines intersect to the surface of the footing. Mark the footing at the point where the plumb bob hits. This is where the corners of the blocks will be laid for the first course.

After all of the corner points have been located, snap a chalk line from one point to the other to outline the wall lines. This will serve as a guide

Drop a plum bob where lines cross to determine corner of block foundation.

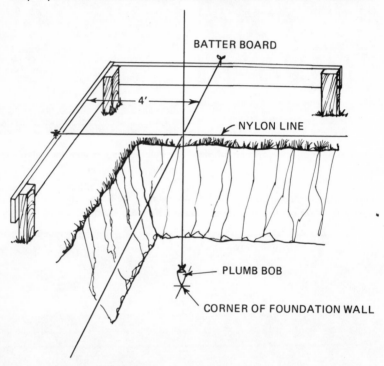

Mark off the lengths of individual blocks on the footing with a pencil and rule. Each block is 16″ long, including the head joint.

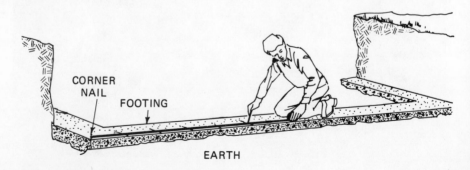

when laying the first course of block on the footing. It also will aid in determining the bond, as each block length can be marked off on the chalk line. Since each standard block, including a mortar head joint, measures 16″, mark off the footing in 16″ increments. If the wall cannot accommodate all full blocks, one block must be cut. Put the cut block in the center of the wall.

The corner block should be laid in a full bed of mortar, without furrowing (see Chapter 5), to assure a waterproof joint. This is done by holding the trowel in a fairly flat position and smoothing the mortar out evenly (see Chapter 5 for detailed instructions on spreading mortar). Level the corner block in both directions. Lay the corner in both directions, three blocks on one side and two on the other. If five blocks are laid, the corner can be built five courses high. This is high enough for most projects. Level the block course by laying the level in the center of the wall lengthwise and tapping the blocks down until true. Plumb the corner block and the end blocks. It is important that the first course is level and plumb, otherwise the entire wall will be crooked. Also, hold the level along the outside face of the blocks and line up the course. This is known as "straightedging."

Next, spread mortar along the edges of the blocks for the bed joint in which to lay the second course. As each block in the second course is laid, check the height with a rule to make sure it is correct. Unless there is a special problem, a block with a ⅜″ mortar bed joint will measure 8″ in height.

HOW TO LAY A CONCRETE-BLOCK CORNER

1. Spread a full bed of mortar for the first course of block.

2. Lay corner block in mortar bed and level it.

3. Apply mortar on the end of a block to form the head joint.

4. After first course has been laid (three blocks in one direction, two in the other), the blocks are leveled . . .

5. . . . and plumbed . . .

6. . . . and aligned.

7. Spread mortar bed on first course of block.

8. As each block in second course is laid, check the height with a mason's rule. Block plus ⅜″ mortar bed should be 8″ high, or #2 on modular rule.

Proper way to lay a block in mortar while holding the trowel. Note how the mason grasps the block in the center of each end in order to maintain balance and keep it level.

To save time, don't put down the trowel every time you lay a block in the mortar bed. Slide the trowel handle into the center of your hand and grip the edges of the block, lifting it onto the mortar bed. Grasp the block at the center when laying it on the mortar bed so it balances well. Set the block down gently. And make sure the edges of the block line up with the one beneath.

Occasionally a block has to be cut to a certain length. If you are too rough with the hammer, the block is not going to break where you want it to. Mark the cut line with the point of the hammer or a pencil. Lay the block on its side and score it gently with the hammer blade all around. Set the block in position and strike the scored line. With luck, the block should break cleanly. If not, gently chip away any excess that projects along the cutting line.

To cut concrete block, score the surface with a hammer at point you want it to break.

Set the block in position and strike the scored line. Block should break cleanly.

When you're ready to lay the third course, attach a line to both ends of the wall with wood blocks. The line should be level with the top edges of the second course. As you lay the third course, keep the top edge of each block about ¹⁄₁₆″ from the line. Each succeeding course of block is laid the same way. Most concrete-block dealers supply wood line blocks with every order.

A concrete-block foundation wall in the process of construction. Corners have been built to five courses, and two courses of center blocks have been laid using a level line supported by blocks.

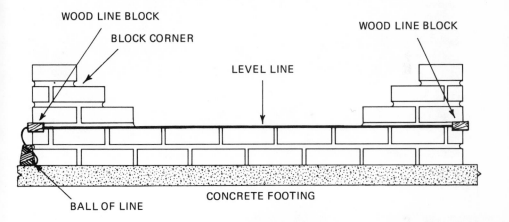

Here a mason builds a foundation wall of concrete block, laying each block to a line stretched the length of the footing.

If block wall needs waterproofing, apply parging mortar with a trowel. Finished wall is shown below. Note sloped cove at bottom to aid drainage.

WATERPROOFING THE FOUNDATION.   If the foundation is going to support a house with a basement, the surface of the block should be waterproofed. Make sure that all protruding mortar is scraped clean and there is no dirt on the surface. Mix a parging mortar of 1 part portland cement to 1 part hydrated lime to 6 parts sand. Add enough water to make a plaster that will be easy to trowel on the wall. (Masonry-cement mortars with special waterproofing agents are available which are good for parging foundations. The choice is up to you.)

You can either parge the block wall with a regular brick trowel or with a rectangular plaster or cement finisher's trowel. The latter works a little better. Before applying any parging mortar, dampen the block with a tank-type garden sprayer so the mortar will not dry out too fast. (You can also use a brush and a bucket of water, but don't soak the wall.) Then, trowel about a ⅜" coat of mortar on the wall, starting at the bottom and working your way to the top. After the parging sets, but has not hardened, scratch it with an old broom so the second coat will adhere to the first coat.

If a tar or mastic waterproofing compound is going to be applied on top of the parging, one ½" coat is all that is necessary. However, let the parging cure a couple of days before applying the tar or mastic. If no tar or mastic is going to be applied, apply two coats of cement to the wall for the best moisture protection. Allow the first coat to cure before applying the second coat.

4 | Bonds and Patterns

To a mason, the term "bond" has three different meanings: (1) the method by which bricks are interlocked, or tied, together so that the entire wall acts as a single structural unit; (2) the pattern that is formed by the bricks and the mortar joints on the face of the wall; (3) the sticking or adhesion of mortar to brick.

Bonds (or patterns) range in design from simple to complex, depending on the preference of the builder. Whichever bond you select for your job, be sure to keep the pattern consistent. If the bond becomes staggered, you won't be happy with the end result.

Three of the most common terms in bricklaying are *head joint, bed joint,* and *course.* A *head joint* is the mortar that is between the ends of the brick; a *bed joint* is the mortar that is under the brick; and a *course* means one layer of brick.

To form the different bonds in masonry walls, the brick must be laid in different positions, and these positions have been given specific names. A bond may be composed of only one brick position which recurs or it may be a combination of several brick positions to form a pattern. These positions are shown in the accompanying drawing.

The two basic joints in bricklaying

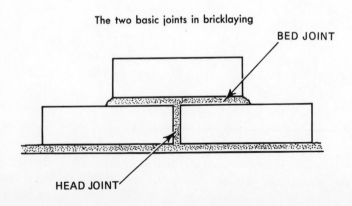

BED JOINT

HEAD JOINT

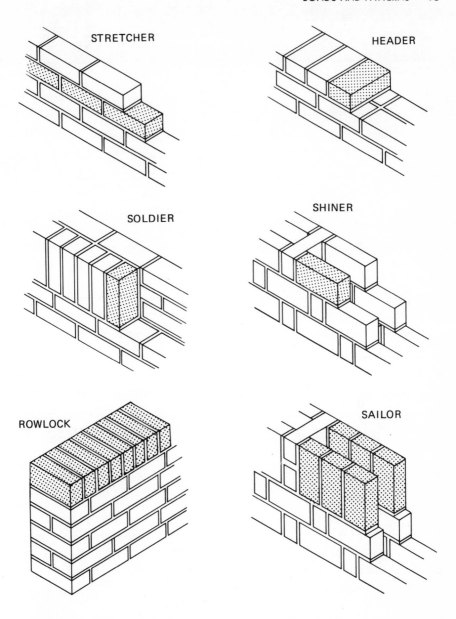

STRETCHER

HEADER

SOLDIER

SHINER

ROWLOCK

SAILOR

The various positions in which bricks may be laid in a wall, with their traditional names.

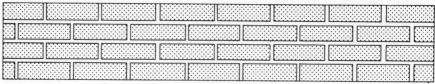

HALF-LAP

RUNNING BOND

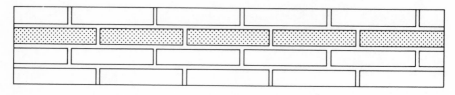

1/3 RUNNING BOND

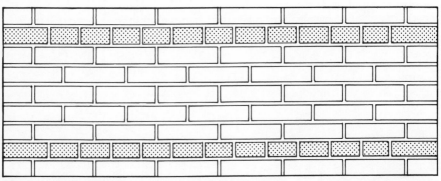

6TH COURSE HEADERS

COMMON BOND

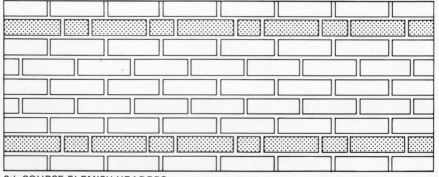

6th COURSE FLEMISH HEADERS

COMMON BOND

Half-lap running bond. The simplest of all bonds is the running or all-stretcher bond. It consists of all full bricks, each laid half over the brick beneath. This is by far the most used bond owing to its simplicity and the fact that few bricks need be cut. The only half bricks used are at the end of the wall.

One-third running bond. There is a variation of the running bond which utilizes a 12″ brick, called a Norman brick. In this bond the 8″ corner brick extends only 4″ over the full brick beneath, causing a one-third lap. This is very popular for facing fireplaces and storefronts.

Common bond with full header. The common, or American, bond is a variation of the running bond with a course of header tie bricks at regular intervals. Usually a common bond wall is backed up with either 4″ or 8″ concrete blocks to a certain height. The brick header is then tied across the wall in mortar resting on the block backing. Header courses usually are laid at either the fifth, sixth, or seventh course, depending on the pattern desired and the height of the block backing. A good use for the common bond would be in a thick, heavy retaining wall to hold back earth. Remember that the header course must be started correctly on the corner with a three-quarter (6″) brick that will lap the required 2″ over the brick beneath.

Common bond with Flemish header. A common-bond brick wall can be varied on the header course by laying what is called a Flemish header. This is only for appearance as both the full header and the Flemish header will tie the wall together strongly enough.

Flemish bond. This bond dates back to early America and was also popular in England. It is still one of the most beautiful of all pattern bonds. Each course of brick consists of alternate stretchers and headers with each header centered over the stretcher brick that is beneath it. The headers in every other course are in a plumb vertical line. Usually a Flemish-bond wall is backed up with brick, as every course is tied into the backing wall. If the wall is to be only a single thickness (4″), headers can be cut in half and the wall bonded together with wall ties or wire reinforcement.

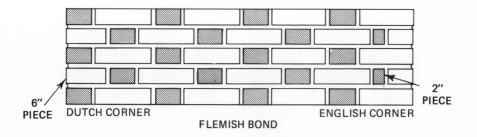

6″
PIECE
DUTCH CORNER
ENGLISH CORNER
2″
PIECE

FLEMISH BOND

There are two methods of starting the corners in a Flemish bond: the Dutch corner, in which a three-quarter (6″) brick is used; and the English corner, in which a 2″ brick is used. The English corner is the traditional method, the Dutch the more modern version. If you are trying to imitate the old Flemish bond, I would recommend the English corner.

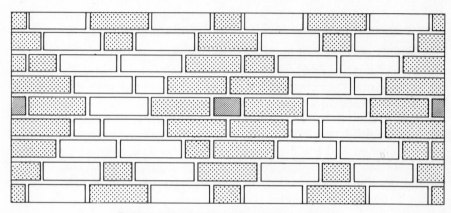

TRIPLE STRETCHER GARDEN WALL BOND

DOUBLE STRETCHER GARDEN WALL BOND
WITH UNITS IN DIAGONAL LINES

STACKED BOND

Double- and triple-stretcher garden-wall bond. Flemish bond can be varied by increasing the number of stretchers between headers in every course. If there are two stretchers between headers, it is called a double-stretcher garden-wall bond. If there are three stretchers between headers on the same course, it is a triple-stretcher garden-wall bond. Close attention must be paid to the placement of every brick in garden-wall bonds as one wrong brick will ruin the pattern. When one looks at a garden-wall bond from a distance, the effect is a diamond pattern. Laying dark headers at predetermined spots will highlight the bond even more.

English bond. English bond is built of alternate courses of headers and stretchers. The headers are centered on the stretchers and joints between stretchers in all courses line up vertically. The English corner and Dutch corner can also be used in this bond.

English cross or Dutch bond. This is a variation of the English bond. Here the vertical joints between stretchers in alternate courses do not line up. These joints center on the stretchers themselves in the courses above and below. The English or Dutch corner can also be used with this bond.

Block or stack bond. In this bond there is no overlapping of bricks. Each brick is laid in line vertically with the one under it. The bricks have to be tied to the backing wall with rigid steel ties to hold them in position. It is also a good idea to lay reinforcement wire in the mortar-bed joint lengthwise every three courses to further strengthen the wall. One of the big problems with stack bond is that all bricks have to be hand picked so they will be close to the same length or you will not be able to keep the vertical head joints the same width.

Paving bonds for brick. Exterior brick paving can be laid in interesting patterns with the different shapes and sizes available. Standard brick is still the favorite, as it lends itself more readily to different patterns and bonds.

There are three basic pattern bonds used in paving work. The others are combinations or variations of these.

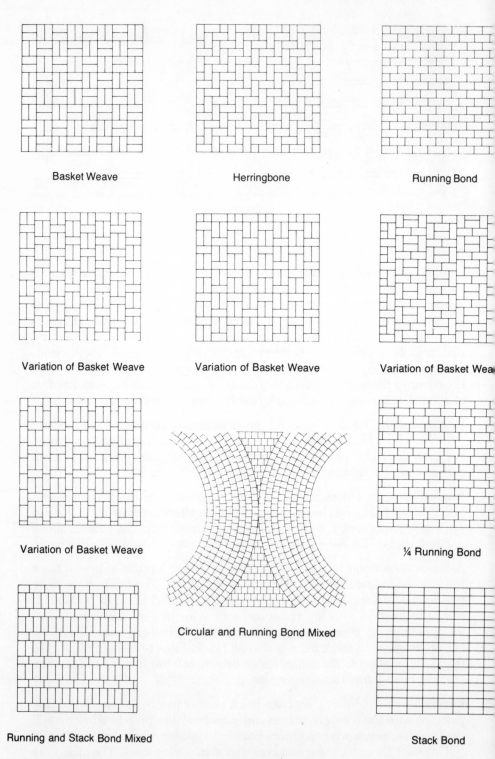

Basket Weave

Herringbone

Running Bond

Variation of Basket Weave

Variation of Basket Weave

Variation of Basket Wea

Variation of Basket Weave

Circular and Running Bond Mixed

¼ Running Bond

Running and Stack Bond Mixed

Stack Bond

BRICK PAVING PATTERNS

Two popular pattern bonds for brick paving, the herringbone (above) and the basketweave.

The *running bond,* which is the same as that used in a wall, is the simplest and easiest to lay. The bricks can be laid in a bed of dry mix or mortar.

The most two popular pattern bonds used for brick paving are the *herringbone* and the *basketweave.* Of all bonds for paving I would recommend the herringbone as it has less likelihood of shifting in place once laid. The basketweave pattern is very pleasing and not as difficult to lay as the herringbone. There is more variation in the size of the joints, however, due to difference in lengths of bricks.

5 | Building a Brick Corner

Almost all brick projects require building an end or corner before laying a wall of bricks. There are three types of corners, or leads, you may have to build. The simplest, known as a *rack-back lead,* is not actually a corner but a number of brick courses built in a straight line and racked back one-half brick on each end until a given height is reached. The first course of a rack-back lead is seldom longer than six bricks, the length of a standard 4' level.

The second type is known as a *straight lead.* It is merely a rack-back lead that is built up square on one end. This is a little tougher to build, as the end must be plumbed along with the face of the lead. A straight lead frequently is built at the end of a wall.

The third type of lead is a *90-degree corner.* It consists of two straight leads joined together. Examples of projects that would need a corner are a barbecue, an enclosing patio wall, or a garage.

The first step is to determine the final height of the wall. This should be figured on the basis of brick courses. Every three courses of standard brick will measure 8" in height including the mortar bed joints, which are

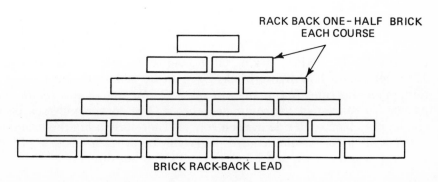

RACK BACK ONE-HALF BRICK
EACH COURSE

BRICK RACK-BACK LEAD

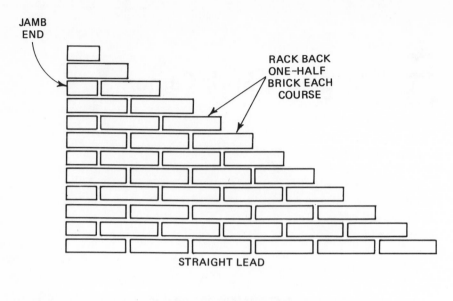

JAMB
END

RACK BACK
ONE-HALF
BRICK EACH
COURSE

STRAIGHT LEAD

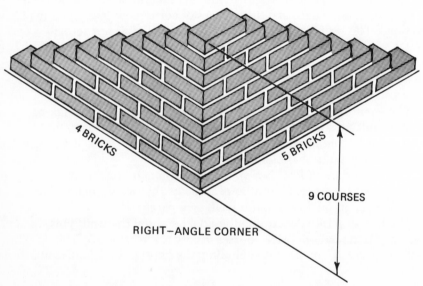

4 BRICKS

5 BRICKS

9 COURSES

RIGHT–ANGLE CORNER

⅜". Using this as a guide, a patio wall, for example, which is to be 24" high, would consist of nine courses. The bricklayer's folding rule, described in Chapter 2, is handy for marking off individual courses on a wood pole.

To determine how many bricks have to be laid in the first course, remember this rule: *The number of bricks in the first course equals the number of courses in the completed corner.* The corner will rack back one-half brick on each side in each course. Therefore, using the example given, a brick corner nine courses high will require a first course of five bricks in one direction and four bricks in the other direction.

Before striking a chalk line on the footing or base, make sure it is brushed free of dirt. Otherwise, bricks will not bond with the mortar. Mark the outline of the corner with a chalk line. I prefer a chalk line, as it is easier to use and can be seen more clearly. First strike a straight line to mark one side of the corner. An accurate method of doing this is to lay a 2′ metal framing square at the point where the corner starts. If you are working by yourself, place two bricks on the end of the line to hold it in place and align it with the blade of the square. Then do the same for the other corner. Always strike the line a little longer than the length of the corner so it won't be concealed by mortar.

1. Using two bricks as a weight, author Dick Kreh strikes chalk line to mark one side of brick corner (right), then, with framing square, establishes right angle and strikes line for other side (below).

2. Finger is used as a spacer for drybonding first course of bricks. Head joints should be ⅜".

Next, drybond the first course of bricks along the chalk line—that is, lay them without mortar to establish proper joint width. This prevents making the head joints too large or too small in the all-important first course. Drybonding is done by inserting your little fingertip between the bricks as a spacer. In most cases this will be about ⅜". Be careful not to insert your finger too far and create too large a head joint. Also be sure to place the best face of the brick to the line, as this will be the face of the corner.

Cutting and spreading mortar. Although there are a variety of methods of cutting mortar from a pan or board, the simplest is called "cupping." It is done in four basic movements and, with a little practice, is not difficult to learn. I recommend that you mix a small batch of mortar and practice cutting and spreading on a base. The skill is important in laying bricks level and keeping them clean.

Hold the trowel so the thumb tip rests slightly behind the bend (white line in photo). This will avoid getting mortar on your thumb (some people are allergic). Don't grip the trowel handle too tightly; your hand may cramp. The accompanying photos show the procedure for cutting and spreading mortar.

3. To cut mortar from main pile, slice down with the trowel and pull a small amount. With a rolling motion, pull the smaller pile to the edge of the board.

4. Shape the mortar into the form of a cigar, or roughly into the shape of the trowel. This will enable you to spread it smoothly, in the correct shape, along the base.

5. Slide the trowel sideways under the mortar. This is done with a quick motion.

6. Pick up the trowel of mortar, snapping your wrist slightly to set the mortar on the blade. Don't snap your wrist too hard or you'll lose the mortar.

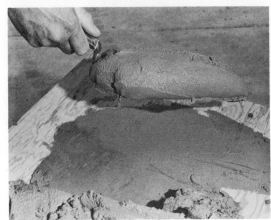

7. Spread the mortar in a sweeping motion, keeping the point of trowel parallel with line. Don't sweep too vigorously or the mortar will not slip off the trowel smoothly. Try not to cover the chalk line.

8. Furrow the mortar bed with the point of the trowel. To do this, hold the trowel at an angle and, with a slight hopping motion, pull it along the bed of mortar, spreading the mortar along the chalk line.

Laying the first course. When you have completed step 8, fill in any irregular places with mortar, being careful not to punch so hard that the tip of the trowel breaks through to the base. Eventually this could cause the joint to leak.

Now you must apply a mortar head joint to the end of a brick.

Hold a brick at roughly a 45-degree angle to the ground and pick up some mortar from the main pile on the end of the trowel. As before, set the mortar on the trowel by giving it a snap. Making sure your fingers are out of the way, swipe downward with the trowel and strike the end of the brick. This will impact the mortar cleanly against the end of the brick, causing it to stick. Although this sounds simple, it will take a little practice to get the right "feel."

Hold the brick with your fingers over the front edge and lay it in the mortar. Don't drop the brick on the mortar; *lay* it down and *press* into position. Then continue laying the rest of the first course.

Once the bricks are laid, lay the level in the center of the course and press down any bricks that are high. If any are low, relay them in fresh mortar. Tap high bricks in the center with the blade of the trowel. Never tap the face lest you chip the brick. Never tap the level itself; you could damage the delicate vials. Plumb and align the bricks as shown in steps 5 and 6 in the photo sequence. Then lay the opposite leg of the corner in mortar.

9. Holding the first brick at about a 45-degree angle to the ground, pick up a small amount of mortar on the trowel, setting it with a slight snap of the wrist.

10. With a downward swipe of the trowel, strike the end of the brick, leaving the mortar in place. The impact of the mortar against the brick causes it to stick.

11. Grasp the brick in the center and lay it in position in the mortar bed, pressing it down gently. Then continue laying the rest of the bricks in the same way.

12. Lay the level in the center of the course and press down any bricks that are too high. If any are low, re-lay them in fresh mortar.

13. Plumb the corner brick by holding the level firmly against its face and resting on the chalk line. Then plumb the other corner brick.

14. Align the entire course by holding the level at the top, outside edge (many bricks have a slight protruding lip there).

The task of keeping the brickwork plumb can be made a lot easier if you stand directly over the bricks as you lay them. Sight down the corner and line the brick you are laying as close as possible with the one beneath in a vertical position. As little as ¼" can be seen readily once you develop this important skill. It will cut down tremendously on the amount of adjustment of the bricks when you plumb the work with the level.

Bricklaying can be made a lot easier if you know where to place your hand when pressing a brick into position. Place your hand flat, so that half extends over the brick previously laid and the other half over the brick being laid. If you don't wear gloves, you'll be able to feel when the brick is level. Cut off the mortar that squeezes out by holding the trowel at a slight angle against the face of the brick. This will prevent smearing the face. When the first course has been laid, leveled, and plumbed, lay the second course, racked back according to the diagram on page 52. As the corner progresses, check the courses with a modular rule. To do this, insert the trowel blade at the bottom of the mortar joint on top of the first course and rest the end of the rule on the blade. Correct spacing for standard bricks, including mortar joints, is number 6 on the scale (see photo). The courses are measured from the first joint because, in leveling the first course, the mortar bed beneath may have been enlarged.

15. Cut off excess mortar at the bottom of the joint and smooth the joint with the tip of the trowel. This stabilizes the course by pressing mortar firmly into the joints.

16. Lay the opposite leg in mortar. If the base is not completely level, it helps to lay the last brick first, as shown here, then fill in the middle ones.

17. When you have laid the opposite leg, spread a bed of mortar on the first course and lay the second course. This is the proper way to position a brick.

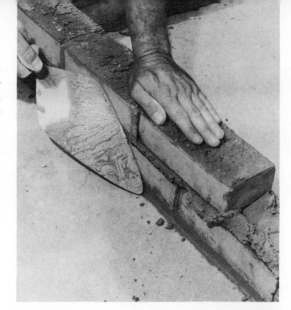

18. To keep the bricks plumb as you proceed, stand directly over the wall and sight from above. A misalignment of ¼ " is noticeable from this position.

19. Check the courses with a modular rule supported on the blade of the trowel. From the base of the bed joint to the top of a brick should measure 6 on the scale.

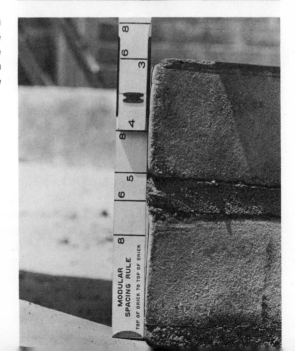

Dry mortar can be restored to workable condition by adding water and mixing with a trowel.

Bricks must be dampened in warm, dry weather. One way is to dip
a brush into a pail of water and flick it over the bricks.

Wetting mortar and bricks. If the weather is warm or dry, mortar will
lose water through being absorbed by the wood mortar board, and by
evaporation. The mortar can be restored to a workable condition by adding water to bring it up to a workable consistency. This is called "temper-
ing" the mortar. Add a little water at a time and mix it with the trowel
or hoe. Be careful not to add so much as to produce a runny mortar which
will be weak. As a rule, mortar should not be tempered more than twice.
Don't mix more mortar than you can use in one hour and you won't have
to temper much.

Bricks, also, must be dampened in warm, dry weather so they won't draw water from the mortar until it has a chance to set. An easy method of dampening bricks is to dip an old brush in a bucket of water and flick it on the bricks. If you have a big pile of bricks, try a fine spray from a garden hose. Be especially careful not to soak the bricks, as they will float on the mortar joint and not set properly. Wet the bricks as often as you feel necessary. If you are having trouble pressing the bricks into their mortar joints, they need wetting.

Tooling the mortar joints. The mortar joints between the bricks should be tooled, or struck, as soon as they are thumbprint hard. This is a simple test which is made by pressing your thumb in the mortar joint. If it leaves an impression, the joint should be tooled immediately. Tooling the mortar joints too soon, when they are wet, will cause smearing or sagging. If you wait too long and the joints set, the metal jointer will produce a black mark on the mortar. This is known as "burning the joints." The joint will not seal against the edges of the brick if it is too stiff, so it is important to tool the joints at the correct time.

When impression of thumb is left in mortar joint, the mortar is ready to be tooled.

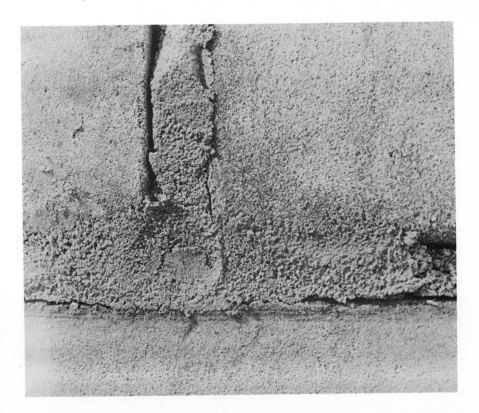

To tool joint, pick up mortar from trowel onto jointer. Pressure causes mortar to stick to tool.

Tool head joints first, holding tool vertically and pressing the curved edge firmly against the mortar.

Tool bed joints by holding tool horizontally. Mortar should fill the gap completely.

The striking tool used here is a round (convex) jointer which will form a half-round impression in the mortar joint, effectively sealing the mortar against the brick. Because of its simplicity, it is by far the most popular joint. To tool the joints, pick up a small amount of mortar on the trowel. Flip the point of the trowel upward so the mortar slides to the rear. Pick up the mortar on the jointer by pressing downward against the trowel and the mortar and at the same time rolling the wrist upward. The pressure will cause the mortar to stick to the jointer.

Always tool the head joints first, before the bed joints. Tooling the head joints first will leave an overrun of the impression in the bed joint. You want the bed joint to be a straight line without imperfections. Thus, you can erase the overruns from the head joints when you tool the bed joints. To tool the head joints, hold the tool vertically and strike with the full part of the curved edge. To tool the bed joints, hold the tool horizontally and press it firmly into the joint so the mortar will fill the joint completely, leaving no gaps along the edges. Retool any joints that are not filled with mortar.

When you've finished tooling the joints, clean the wall with a medium-stiff brush. A long-handled stove brush, sold in most hardware stores, is a good choice. Allow the tooled mortar joints enough time to surface dry before brushing or they may smear.

When the mortar is partially dry, brush wall and remove excess.

Tooling a wall with a rake-out jointer.

Tailing the corner with a level. If any brick between the first and last courses are out of line, tap them into line with trowel handle.

The completed corner.

Rake-out joints. There are a number of different types of joints that can be tooled in a brick wall. A rake-out joint, for example, is attractive on a fireplace or barbecue. Use the rake-out jointer shown in Chapter 2. Set the nail no more than ⅜" below the bottom of the wheels and tighten the thumbscrew. The wheels straddle the joint while the nail rakes the mortar. Brush out the joints when you have finished raking them. Rake-out joints give a wall a feeling of depth, and reveal the real beauty of the bricks.

Checking and "tailing" the corner. After the corner has been built, it is a good idea to recheck the height with the mason's rule. Lay the trowel flat on the top, corner brick, its edge projecting slightly. Hold the rule as before, even with the top of the first course. The blade should cut the rule at number 6.

Finally, check the ends of the racked-back bricks to be sure they align. This is called "tailing" the corner. Hold the level as shown in the photo at left. If any bricks between the first and last courses are out of line, tap them into line with the trowel handle. Don't adjust the top and bottom bricks. After adjusting the bricks, restrike any mortar joints that are cracked or loose. Tailing the corner is important. If the bricks in the corner are aligned and plumbed correctly, only minor adjustments will have to be made as the wall is built.

Practice corner-building until you have learned how to keep the bricks plumb and aligned. Don't become discouraged. If a corner starts to get out of plumb, stop at that point, remove the course and relay the bricks properly. Once a corner gets out of plumb, and the mortar has set, there is no way to fix it. Take your time and give the corner the care it deserves.

6 | Laying Bricks to the Line

As long as the wall you are building is less than 48″ long, you can use a mason's level to align the bricks. But, if you want to build a wall that is longer, a line must be used or else the bricks will be hopelessly crooked. This is normal, as not even a professional bricklayer can build a long, straight wall without a line as a guide.

You could use a long, straight board as a guide, but this is more trouble than it is worth. The correct way is to build a corner or straight lead, whichever is needed, at both ends of the wall and attach a line to the wall.

The photos in this chapter show how to lay bricks to the line. Although principally the laying of bricks to the line is shown, the same techniques apply to laying any masonry material to the line.

After drybonding the first course, lay the end brick in mortar; level and plumb it.

Stretch a line from end brick to corner, using line blocks, and lay first course to the line.

To place line block, tie a knot in the end of line and slip line in the groove. Set a block on each corner, the line flush with the course of brick to be laid.

If it is not feasible to use line blocks, use nail and steel pin driven into each end of wall.

Sometimes when building a long wall, the line tends to sag. It can be supported in the middle of the wall with a metal clip called a trig, which is held in place beneath a brick.

Left: Lay the bricks to the line, pressing them down and cutting off the excess mortar that squeezes out with the trowel blade.

Below: As can be seen in this top view, bricks should be laid about 1/16 inch from the line, just so daylight can be seen between line and brick.

The last brick laid in the course is called the "closure" brick. To prevent the joints from leaking, it is a good practice to butter all four edges with mortar and then lay the brick in position.

1. Mark the brick where it is to be cut with a pencil and small square.

2. Holding the brick with fingers well below the edge, score the pencil line with edge of a brick hammer. Strike lightly so as not to break the brick.

3. Turn the brick and score it on all surfaces. Then strike the scored line on the face. The brick should break along the line.

4. Chip off any bumps to make a clean, neat cut.

To cut with a brick chisel, lay the brick on a piece of wood to cushion the blow. With the flat side of the chisel facing the piece to be used, strike a sharp blow with the hammer. The brick should break clean.

7 | Building a Brick Wall Around Basement Entrance

One of the problems with development homes is inadequate drainage along the sides, usually the result of improper grading. This can be especially critical if the house has an entranceway to the basement that fills up with water after a heavy rain. Although a drain at the base of the step will carry off some water, it rarely can keep the place dry. In no time at all, the basement is flooded, causing damage to the house.

A cure for the problem is to build a brick wall around the entranceway, then regrade the area so the ground slopes away from the wall.

In the example shown in this chapter (my brother's home), the entranceway had an existing concrete wall on which a brick wall could be built. The concrete wall served, in effect, as a footing for the brick wall. After we

Concrete areaway looked like this before work began. As the top landing was lower than the existing grade, water ran down the steps when it rained.

Laying the first course of brick around the iron railing. The wall was two bricks thick.

built the wall, we spread a truckload of dirt around the wall, grading it so water would drain away from the house. Then we planted grass. With most of the runoff water diverted, the drain at the bottom of the steps could handle the natural rainfall.

Once we determined the number of bricks needed for the job, they were ordered from a local building supplier. Bricks were selected that matched the house. The bricks were then stocked around the areaway, leaving enough room to get in and work.

Masonry-cement mortar was mixed in the wheelbarrow, as described in Chapter 2. The existing concrete wall had an iron railing around it to prevent anyone from falling into the entranceway. We decided to leave this in place and lay brick around it, as it would serve as a reinforcement for the wall. It was necessary to cut some of the bricks to fit around the railing. The gaps were filled with mortar.

The first course was laid dry, to establish the bond and attempt to build the wall of full bricks with no cuts. The mortar joints were spaced approximately ⅜″ apart, which is standard head-joint width.

After drybonding was completed, a brick was laid, leveled, and plumbed at each end of the wall and a line attached. The first course, the front of the wall, was laid in mortar; then the inside, backing course was laid in the same manner.

Building the brick corner. To stabilize the railing, we filled the space behind the backing course with mortar.

Preparing to lay the rowlock course across the entrance.

Swiping a mortar joint on the side of a rowlock brick.

The completed mortar joint as it should appear on the brick.

Tapping the closure rowlock brick in place. Mortar should squeeze out from all edges to insure a full, leakproof joint.

Next, one corner was built up to wall height—to No. 6 on the modular rule. To prevent water from running down the steps, two courses of brick were laid at the top of the stairway—a rowlock and a header course. The rowlock course was laid across the opening to meet the concrete stub on the opposite side.

It was important that the mortar joints between the rowlock bricks were well filled, to keep water out. To assure a tight joint, we buttered the mortar directly onto the brick with the trowel rather than trying to apply it to the head joint after the brick had been laid.

The last brick laid in a course—the closure brick—is the one most likely to leak, so it should be buttered well with mortar; also the ends of the two in-place bricks. The mortar should squeeze out of the joint as the brick is pressed into position.

Checking the finished brickwork at entranceway with the level.

Building the corner adjacent to the rowlock course.

The finished wall. Earth was filled in and grass seed planted.

When the rowlock and header courses were laid and plumbed, we sealed all holes where the brickwork met the concrete base and struck and brushed the work.

Then we built the other corner to the correct height. A short level came in handy when working around the railing. We struck the mortar joints as soon as they stiffened, so as not to smear them. This can be checked by pressing the thumb into the mortar joint. If the thumb leaves only a damp impression, the joints are ready to be struck.

Once the corners were built, we laid the brick wall to the line. We ordered a truckload of earth and filled in around the wall after it had cured. To complete the job, we planted grass seed.

8 | Retaining Walls

A retaining wall is a wall that is built to restrain earth or some type of fill. It is subjected to more pressure than a regular wall and therefore should either be strengthened with steel rods or metal joint reinforcement, or built wider at the base. A retaining wall must also contain some means of draining off water that otherwise would build up pressure of sufficient force to damage the wall.

Retaining walls can be built of concrete block, brick, or stone, depending on the appearance desired. A brick wall backed by concrete block is popular because of its simplicity and ease of construction. Stone looks good but is more difficult for the average handyman to work with, especially if laid in mortar. The typical retaining wall around a home rarely exceeds 4′ in height. Walls higher than 4′ pose special problems and should be built by a professional.

A retaining wall is subjected to severe stress from moisture and pressure. Therefore, for best results a strong mortar should be used—either Type M or S. You can obtain masonry-cement mortars or mix portland cement and lime to attain the same strength. Mortar plays an important part in the strength of the retaining wall. Before starting the job, however, consider the problems that dictate building the wall. For example, if there has been a lot of ground water washing down a slope, check to see if rainspouts are emptying into the area. This could be corrected by laying pipes in the ground from the downspouts, to drain away the water. Examine the slope of the ground to determine if there is a natural depression that causes water to drain into the area. You may want to dig a ditch to change the course of the water. In other words, look the situation over and try to remedy the water problems first. There is no point in building a retaining wall only to have it crack and lean a year later. The second time around, the job is going to be very difficult, as you will have to clean up the old wall before building a new one.

There are two general types of masonry retaining walls. One, called a gravity wall, is built wider at the bottom than at the top. The mass and

Concrete-block retaining wall with brick cap is dangerously weak and could collapse at any time. Cause is lack of drainage, allowing pressure to build up behind the wall.

Gravity retaining wall.

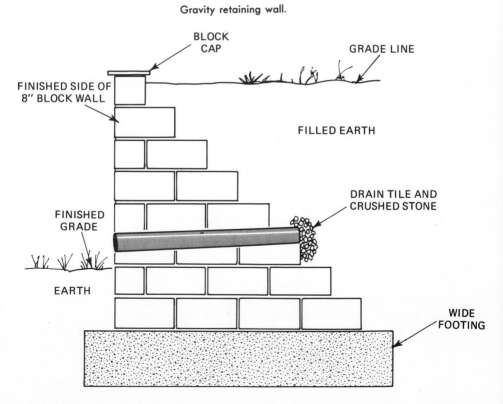

BLOCK CAP

GRADE LINE

FINISHED SIDE OF 8" BLOCK WALL

FILLED EARTH

DRAIN TILE AND CRUSHED STONE

FINISHED GRADE

EARTH

WIDE FOOTING

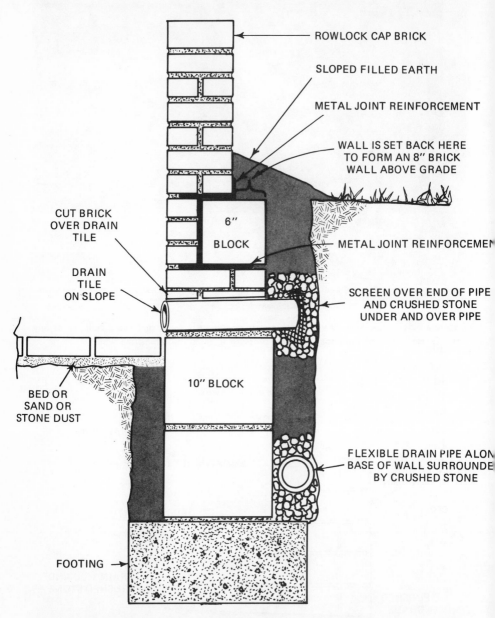

ROWLOCK CAP BRICK

SLOPED FILLED EARTH

METAL JOINT REINFORCEMENT

WALL IS SET BACK HERE
TO FORM AN 8" BRICK
WALL ABOVE GRADE

CUT BRICK
OVER DRAIN
TILE

6"
BLOCK

METAL JOINT REINFORCEMEN

DRAIN
TILE
ON SLOPE

SCREEN OVER END OF PIPE
AND CRUSHED STONE
UNDER AND OVER PIPE

10" BLOCK

BED OR
SAND OR
STONE DUST

FLEXIBLE DRAIN PIPE ALON
BASE OF WALL SURROUNDE
BY CRUSHED STONE

FOOTING

Concrete-block-and-brick retaining wall, cross section. Pressure is relieved by building drain tile into the wall slightly above grade line. Flexible drain pipe along base also draws off water.

weight at the bottom of the wall give it extra strength. The other type is straight-sided, but strengthened with reinforcements.

Let's look at the procedure for building a typical reinforced retaining wall. A friend of mine wanted to build a patio at the end of his house. There was a dirt bank on each side of the house so it was necessary to build two retaining walls. As there was not a great deal of earth fill, we decided

Area at rear of house where patio was to be laid and protected by retaining walls.

to build two 10″ wide, concrete-block-and-brick reinforced walls. A drain line of perforated plastic tiles extended from the house foundation; it would be extended along the walls to drain water. We laid the drain tiles in a 2″ bed of crushed stone. A rigid (tile) 4″ × 12″ drain tile was enclosed in the brick wall to relieve moisture build-up, and a nonrusting-type screen was laid against the back of the drain tile and held in place with crushed stone.

A foundation had to be installed. We dug a trench 2′ deep, which would put the foundation below the frost line. Then we drove small metal stakes into the bottom of the trench to serve as level points when pouring the concrete footing. The footing was then poured into the trench and allowed to cure.

Two courses of 10″ concrete blocks were needed to bring the wall up

First course of block was laid on footing, which was poured directly into trench without forms.

Concrete-block foundation for retaining wall was built up to the grade line. Earth was then filled around the wall before laying bricks on the block.

Brickwork laid out with drain tiles installed through the wall.

Laying bricks to a line, I reach the level of the concrete-block wall with the sixth course.

to grade height. We stretched a line from the corner of the building to the wall line stake and laid out the wall in mortar. It is important to have a full bed of mortar on the first course to provide good bearing and a waterproof joint. Two courses of block were then laid to the top of the trench.

The bricks were drybonded on the face side of the block wall and then laid in mortar.

The brick corners were built up first. We used a long 2×4, laid from corner to corner, to support the level. Bricks were laid to a line stretched between the corners.

Four-inch-diameter drain tiles 12″ long were laid on top of the first course of brick to provide drainage through the wall. We surrounded the drain tiles on the outside of the wall with crushed stone, to prevent the earth from silting in over the pipe. It is also a good idea to install a piece of nonrusting screen or mesh wire over the end of the pipe so the stones do not come through. The drain tiles were laid in the wall on a slight slope so the water would be able to run through readily. When the brick wall reached the level of the block wall, metal reinforcement was laid in the mortar joints. We installed this reinforcement every three courses of brick.

Metal joint reinforcements tie both walls together and provide additional strength.

Building the brick return of the wall. Since the grade on this side was low, the block was faced with brick on both sides.

The last rowlock course is laid. Note how the wall was built in steps to match the existing grade.

The completed wall.

The end of the wall was given a corner return for extra strength and to provide a surface on which to set a wood corner post. My friend planned to build a roof over the patio later so it could be used in rainy weather.

Since the ground behind the house was sloped, we stepped the wall to conform generally to this grade. The last course of brick was laid in rowlock style. When the wall had cured sufficiently, earth was filled behind it to match the grade of the yard.

TREE PROTECTION. A tree's roots must have air, water, and minerals. When the grade of the ground is changed, increasing or decreasing the amount of soil over the root area, the roots will have difficulty obtaining these important nutrients. Therefore, it is necessary to protect the tree. A properly designed and constructed brick retaining wall will do the job.

An attractive type of retaining wall is the circular tree well. To lay out the well, use a length of garden hose to mark the circle around the tree to be excavated. Dig a trench about a foot deep and pour a concrete footing for the wall.

If the diameter of the wall is large enough, it can be laid out with

A circular tree well built of decorative bricks.

A circular brick retaining wall built around a tree to raise the grade.

stretcher bricks. But if the diameter is 4' or less, you will have to build the wall of headers. Build the wall about one course higher than the proposed grade line and cap off with a rowlock or header course. When the wall is finished, fill around the edge with topsoil. Pour about 3" of gravel into the bottom of the well.

Another example of how a retaining wall can be used to protect a tree is shown in the accompanying photo. When my father-in-law built his house, there was a beautiful dogwood tree where he wanted to build a patio. The existing grade had to be excavated to meet the sill of the basement door. If we did not make some special provisions, the tree would have to be cut down and removed. The solution was to build a circular brick retaining wall around the tree and enclose the root system. To give the wall an attractive design, we omitted the head joints between the bricks. The top was capped with flagstone.

These circular retaining walls are two examples of how you can save a tree. Minor fills of earth, 12" or less in depth, will not harm most trees, but any major change in grade level will require some type of retaining wall if the tree is to survive.

9 | Planters and Garden Pools

If you want to enhance your grounds consider building a brick planter and fountain. Both can add charm to a patio or garden.

Masonry planters can be round, square or free-form. No hard and fast rules apply to their design. You may decide to build dry with fieldstone, or you may prefer laying brick, block or stone in mortar.

Before settling on a design for a planter, it's a good idea to consider what you're going to plant in it, and what the requirements will be. For example, if flowers are to grow well, they'll need plenty of sun and water. Don't build your planter in a shaded area or close to a large tree whose roots will absorb most of the water. The walls of the planter should be strong enough to withstand the pressure of the soil it encloses. Also, remember that a planter will be subject to moisture and cold. Metal joint reinforcement and a strong mortar will make the walls more resistant.

Two brick planters, flanking a brick barbecue, enhance the author's patio and help to retain the paving stones.

Circular brick planter built in a well motif is an original and challenging project.

This rectangular planter was built to match the fall in the grade of the lawn.

Cross section of planter shows details of construction.

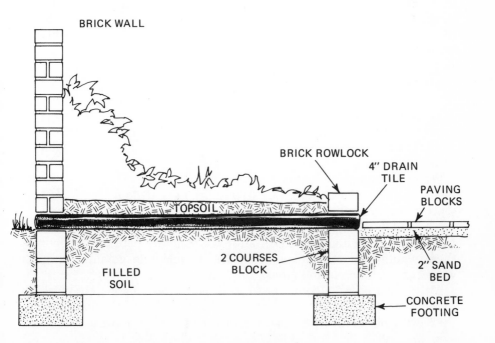

BRICK WALL

BRICK ROWLOCK

4" DRAIN TILE

PAVING BLOCKS

TOPSOIL

2 COURSES BLOCK

FILLED SOIL

2" SAND BED

CONCRETE FOOTING

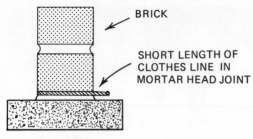

BRICK

SHORT LENGTH OF
CLOTHES LINE IN
MORTAR HEAD JOINT

SIDE VIEW

Short lengths of clothes line were inserted in the head joints of planter wall. Pulled out before mortar hardened, they left drain holes to relieve pressure.

A few small drain holes at the bottom of the walls will help to relieve any pressure that builds up from moisture. These are easily created by inserting short lengths of clothes line in the mortar head joints and pulling them out before the mortar hardens. If you soak the lengths of line in motor oil beforehand, they'll withdraw easily.

The next consideration is a good foundation. Like any other outdoor masonry structure, it will have to go below the frost line. Dig a trench where the wall will be built and pour no less than 4″ of concrete for the footing.

I built two brick planters on my patio that not only serve as flower beds but also retain the paving. The front brick wall is low, the back wall approximately 3′ high. The planters are about 4′ wide, allowing ample room to plant shorter-growing flowers in the front and taller ones in the back.

Since the planters were designed to project into the patio area, provision had to be made to drain water from hard rains. I accomplished this by putting 4″ diameter drain tiles in the wall, at floor level, which ran completely through the wall and flower bed.

For the patio floor, I cast 2″-thick concrete-and-gravel paving blocks in a 2×4 wood frame. The paving blocks were laid in a bed of stone screening (also called stone dust) with a 2″ sand topping bed.

BUILDING A GARDEN POOL. There is something refreshing about a garden pool with a fountain. On a warm summer evening it is pleasant to sit on the patio, sipping a cool drink, and listen to the gentle trickle of water.

When I designed my patio, I decided to build a pool with a fountain in the corner. After evaluating various designs, I decided on giving the pool a brick border wall and making the fountain of natural rubble stone.

I started by excavating an area 2′ deep where the pool was to be built. I wanted it deep enough so that after the concrete bottom was poured, there would be room for enough water to maintain goldfish. The fish would control insects and amuse the children.

Next, I poured a 6″ footing and laid three courses of concrete block up to the grade line. For extra strength, I placed steel reinforcement wire in the mortar joints of every course. A few strips of wire mesh laid in the mortar

Attractive garden pool in author's yard is built of brick and stone. Small electric pump circulates water continuously from pool to fountain.

Footing for pool was poured into 2' excavation. Three courses of concrete block, strengthened with steel reinforcement and wire mesh, were laid to grade level.

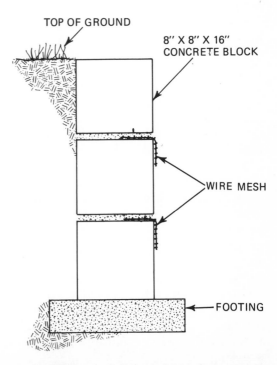

TOP OF GROUND

8" X 8" X 16" CONCRETE BLOCK

WIRE MESH

FOOTING

joints were left projecting into the pool area to help reinforce the concrete that was later poured for the pool liner.

The brickwork was laid in running bond. I used Type S masonry-cement mortar to be sure the joints would be waterproof. The rear wall was built 2' high, to serve as the support for the stonework. The last course on the

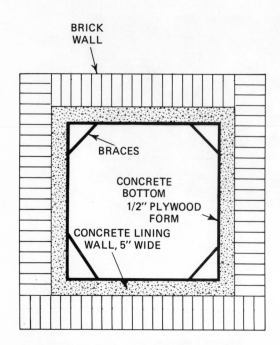

BRICK
WALL

BRACES

CONCRETE
BOTTOM
1/2" PLYWOOD
FORM
CONCRETE LINING
WALL, 5" WIDE

Brick enclosure is lined with 5" wall of concrete. Wall was poured into plywood form, built 10" smaller than interior of wall.

wall was a rowlock. I also laid metal joint reinforcement in the brickwork every three courses for extra strength. This metal reinforcement is available from building-supply dealers everywhere. One well-known brand is called DUR-O-WAL masonry wall reinforcement. It comes in 10' lengths and different widths, with $\frac{3}{16}$" diameter wire that can easily be cut with wire cutters.

On the two remaining walls that fronted the patio, one stretcher course was laid and capped with a rowlock course above grade level.

The next step was to build a wood form inside the pool area to hold the concrete lining. I made a square box of ½" plywood 24" tall and 10" smaller than the brick enclosure, which would give me a 5" lining wall. I mixed the concrete for the bottom first—1 part portland cement to 3 parts gravel—and poured it about 6" thick, placing wire reinforcement as the concrete was poured. Then I set the wood form on the concrete floor and poured the lining walls, to form a watertight unit. Before pouring, I nailed a small strip of wood across each corner of the form to brace it and prevent it from twisting out of square. After the concrete was poured, I tapped the sides of the form lightly with a hammer in order to eliminate any holes or voids which would appear after the form was removed. I allowed the concrete to cure two days before removing the forms with a wrecking bar.

I built the waterfall of natural rubble stone which would not require any special tools or cutting. The top of the concrete lining wall was 4" below the front rowlock course, allowing room to lay stone that would come almost flush with the bricks. I chose a large, flat stone, somewhat triangular in shape, for the base of the waterfall. The stone was laid up in a mortar

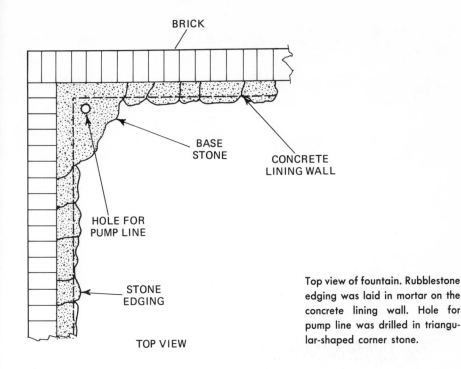

BRICK

BASE STONE

CONCRETE LINING WALL

HOLE FOR PUMP LINE

STONE EDGING

TOP VIEW

Top view of fountain. Rubblestone edging was laid in mortar on the concrete lining wall. Hole for pump line was drilled in triangular-shaped corner stone.

mix of 1 part portland cement, ¼ part hydrated lime, and 3 parts sand. This is high-strength mortar, Type M, which adheres well to stone.

A hole was left at the rear of the triangular corner stone for the pump's water line, and I inserted a length of 1″ plastic hose into the stonework.

The stones were laid in random style with no cutting, merely fitting them in the mortar so the edges would show. The top stone was naturally dished in the shape of a bowl. I wanted some of the water that was pumped up from the bottom of the pool to fill the dished stone and then run down the small wall of stones like a waterfall.

To make the mortar joints look rustic and natural, I used a short length of old broom handle with a rounded end to rake out the joints between the stones. Then I brushed the stonework with a medium-stiff-bristle brush.

At a local garden-supply shop I bought a small electric recirculating pump and a concrete ornamental statue with a hole in it. To hook up the pump I inserted its ½″ plastic hose into the 1″ hose I had built into the stonework, the end of which fit into the base of the statue. The pump was placed on the bottom of the pool and its cord plugged into a nearby outlet. Water was pumped from the pool to the fountain and returned via the waterfall. Occasionally I had to add more water to the pool to make up for that lost through evaporation and absorption.

In cold weather, when the fountain is not in use, I drop a short log of wood in the water. The wood absorbs the pressure created by the freezing and thawing water and prevents the pool walls from cracking.

10 | Brick Walks

There are two basic ways of laying a brick walk: in a dry mix of stone screenings and sand topping; or in a bed of mortar on a concrete slab. Either way, this is a relatively easy project and the materials are not expensive.

I prefer laying bricks in a dry mixture, for I have found that when they are laid in mortar on a concrete base they eventually will crack, unless covered by a roof. This is caused by contraction and expansion due to freezing and thawing. Simply put, mortarless paving is faster, cheaper, and easier to lay.

A brick walk laid in sand, stone screenings, or a combination of each will require little maintenance over the years. It will stretch with the weather. After the bricks have been laid in position, either sand or a mixture of sand and dry portland cement is swept into the joints. If it washes out in time, it is easily replaced.

MATERIALS. For the walk itself, use hard bricks with no holes, called pavers, which are available from building-supply dealers. The base can be made of regular building sand, stone screenings, or fine crushed stone. Stone screenings, if available, are an excellent base. Usually a 1″ or 2″ bed of sand is spread on top to keep the stone dust in place. A few bags of portland cement and some wood 2×4s for form boards and stakes complete the list of materials.

To determine the number of bricks needed for pavings, first find the area of the walk. (For example, if the walk measures 3′ by 24′, the area would of course be 72 square feet.) There are 4.5 standard bricks to each square foot of walk. Multiplying 72 feet by 4.5, gives you 324 bricks. Allow a few dozen extra for the border and for broken bricks. Roughly 400 bricks should do the job.

The sand and stone screenings are figured by rule of thumb measurement; that is, 1 ton of sand or stone dust, approximately 2″ deep, will cover about 100 square feet. You'll need some sand left over to sweep in the joints between the bricks, but this would not be a large amount. For our 72-square-foot walk, it would be safe to estimate that a ton of stone screenings or sand would do the job.

The amount of portland cement needed would have to be determined by how much is added to the dry mix and how much is used to sweep into the joints. About two bags would do for this job. As a rule, your building-supply dealer will be able to give you an estimate of materials. This is one of the services he provides.

PREPARING THE BASE. You will need a good base with sufficient drainage if the walk is to last without settling or shifting. Drive stakes at each end of the proposed walk and stretch lines to demark the edges. Keep the lines high enough so as not to interfere with the digging. In most cases I recommend excavating the walk area to a depth of 8″ with a pick, mattock, and shovel. If grass is present it might be a good idea to cut out the sod and use it somewhere else.

After the walkway has been excavated to the desired depth, drive stakes into the ground a 2×4's width from the edges. Then nail 2×4s (select straight ones) to the stakes and level each side with the other. These will serve as a form for laying the brick.

Attach line to two wood stakes to mark excavation for the walk.

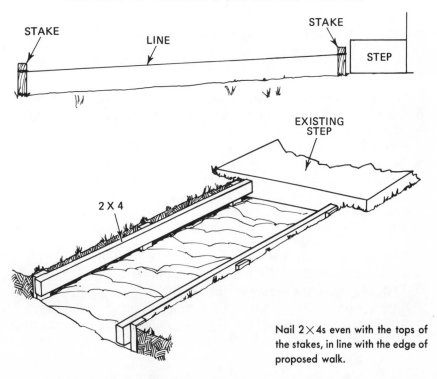

STAKE
STAKE
LINE
STEP

EXISTING STEP

2 X 4

Nail 2×4s even with the tops of the stakes, in line with the edge of proposed walk.

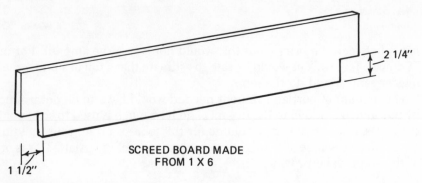

2 1/4"

1 1/2"

SCREED BOARD MADE
FROM 1 X 6

Wood screed board used for leveling dry bed materials. Select reasonably straight board and notch with saw as shown.

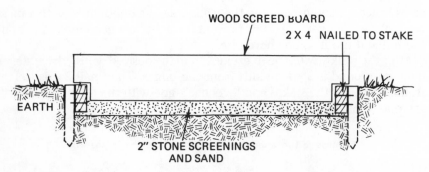

WOOD SCREED BOARD

2 X 4 NAILED TO STAKE

EARTH

2" STONE SCREENINGS
AND SAND

Screed board in position on 2×4 wood form boards. Board is dragged across the 2×4s to level the bed.

Next, cut a wood screed board from a 1×6. This will be used for leveling the stone screening and sand to the right height. Notch the board to allow for the thickness of the brick (2¼") that will be laid on the bed.

Shovel in the dry mix and screed off, tamping firmly with a rake or flat object. If it settles, add a little more and rescreed until the depth is right.

If you want to install an edging course, now is the time to do it. An edging course helps to hold the walk in place. Here I used bricks laid on edge against the 2×4 form. You will have to rake out a little dry mix from under the edging bricks to level them with the pavers. Tamp them down firmly with a hammer handle. Lay the bricks tightly against each other.

A slight crown can be built into the walk if additional drainage is needed. This is done by keeping the bricks in the center slightly higher and tapering from the center to the sides.

You can experiment with one of the more advanced bonds, such as the herringbone, or use the traditional paving bond, which is running bond. The nice part about this work is you can be your own designer. I selected running bond for the paving.

Brick edging laid against 2×4 form board.

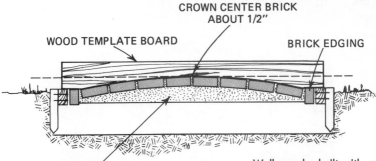

CROWN CENTER BRICK
ABOUT 1/2"

WOOD TEMPLATE BOARD

BRICK EDGING

STONE
SCREENINGS
AND SAND

Walk can be built with crown in center to drain water more effectively. Cut a wood template to the curvature desired and rest it on the 2×4s. Lay bricks to meet the bottom of the template.

Laying brick in running bond. Make sure all bricks are settled firmly in sand bed by tapping down with hammer handle.

The walk was first drybonded. A half brick was cut at the ends of every other course to provide a half lap. Lay the bricks tightly against each other, tapping them firmly into the dry-mix bed with the hammer handle. At the completion of bricklaying, gently remove the 2×4 form board and stakes and fill in with dirt, tamping well to support the brick border.

Sweep a dry mixture of 1 part portland cement to 4 parts sand into the joints. To complete the job, dampen the walk with a fine spray from a garden hose or watering can. As time passes, it may be necessary to sweep more sand into the joints due to losses from rain or movement.

In time, there will probably be some weed growth between the joints. This can be slowed by periodically spraying with weed killer. Black plastic can be laid under the brick to control weed growth, but plastic will break down after a period of time, and I don't think it's worth the time and effort. If properly installed the walk will last a long time without any maintenance.

The completed walk.

Laying brick in a mortar bed. A brick walk laid in a mortar bed must have a concrete base. The base should be at least 4″ thick and reinforced with wire.

After the concrete has cured, the procedure is much the same as for mortarless paving, except mortar is used in place of the dry-mix bed.

I recommend a flat-tooled joint on all paving work so water does not lay in the joint and cause the mortar to deteriorate. Strike the mortar joints as soon as they're thumbprint hard.

Establishing two level bricks by using a 2×4 straightedge with level laid on top.

Laying bricks in the walk to a line.

11 | Laying a Brick Patio

Although patios can be made of many materials, we will be concerned in this chapter with brick. One of the advantages of brick is that it lends itself to a variety of colors and bonds. Also, the relative ease of cutting and fitting bricks makes them a popular choice.

Cross section of retaining wall built to contain patio shown in this chapter. Earth fill was covered with bed of gravel and sand, and pavings laid within the brick rowlock border.

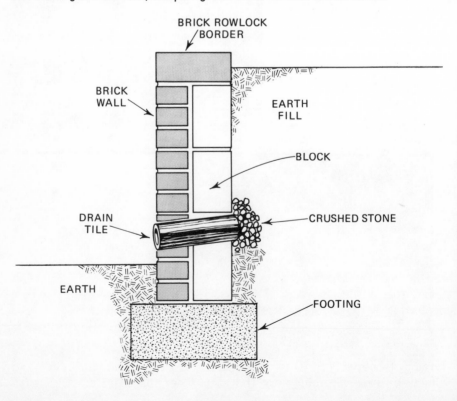

BRICK ROWLOCK BORDER

BRICK WALL

EARTH FILL

BLOCK

DRAIN TILE

CRUSHED STONE

EARTH

FOOTING

High retaining walls are often built to enclose a patio and hold the pavings. Drain tiles were built into this wall.

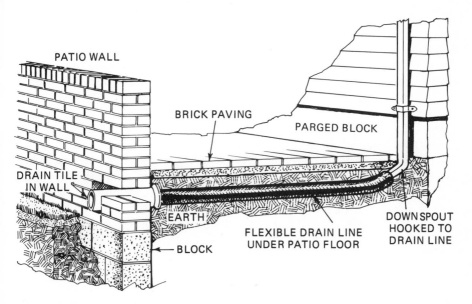

PATIO WALL

BRICK PAVING

PARGED BLOCK

DRAIN TILE IN WALL

EARTH

DOWNSPOUT HOOKED TO DRAIN LINE

FLEXIBLE DRAIN LINE UNDER PATIO FLOOR

BLOCK

To provide for adequate drainage, flexible drain line can be run from downspout, under patio floor, to drain tile in retaining wall.

For a patio, select a hard paver brick in a suitable color. You can either lay the bricks in sand or in mortar. As we noted in the last chapter, bricks laid outdoors in mortar tend to crack from the freezing and thawing that occur during harsh winters. Of course, if you live in a warm climate, this will not be a problem. If you live in a region where the winters are cold, by all means lay the bricks in sand.

Drainage. When you lay a masonry surface on the ground, it is going to affect the natural drainage of the area. Therefore, you have to make

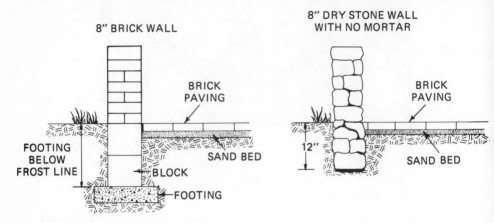

Cross section of typical brick and stone walls for retaining brick paving.

provisions for drainage. Normally, if the paving surface is given a slight slope, excess water will run off. But if you live in a region of heavy rainfall, it may be advisable to dig a few trenches, before laying the patio floor, and install a couple of lines of drain tile to carry away excess water. Cover the tile joints with strips of tar paper, to keep out dirt, and finally cover the tiles with a layer of crushed stone.

You will have to build some type of border wall around the patio to contain the paving, and it, too, must be equipped for drainage. The patio shown here was built on a terraced slope; a brick retaining wall was built before any paving bricks were laid. Drain tiles were installed through the wall two courses of brick above grade. This was important as the retaining wall supported a heavy load of earth and would have cracked under pressure without adequate drainage. If rain spouts empty into the patio area, it is advisable to run flexible drain lines through the drain tiles. A tremendous amount of water collects on a roof and should be carried away from the patio.

LAYING BRICKS IN SAND.   First, fill in the paving area with gravel or stone screenings, finishing with about a 2″ topping of sand. The gravel should be packed firmly with a tamper and additional material added to bring the base to the correct height.

The brick will be laid slightly higher than the top of the border and tapped firmly in the bed with the handle of a brick hammer or a rubber mallet. The most common method of laying bricks on sand is with closed joints, pressed tightly together. When the bricks have been laid, sand is swept into the spaces between the joints.

Herringbone bond was selected for this patio. Once we got the bond underway, the kids helped to lay the bricks. It was simply a matter of following the pattern and making sure the bricks were tapped firmly in

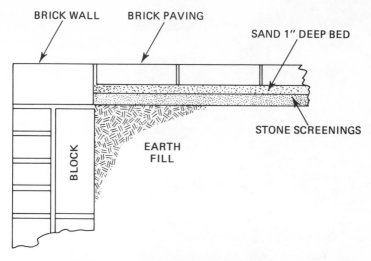

BRICK WALL   BRICK PAVING   SAND 1" DEEP BED

STONE SCREENINGS

BLOCK   EARTH FILL

Cross section of brick paving on sand-and-stone screenings.

After retaining wall was built, and a gravel base laid, sand was distributed in the patio area and tamped.

Laying brick pavings in a herringbone pattern is a job even children can do.

Checking the leading edge of the pavings with a 2×4 to be sure they're aligned.

Surest way to align bricks is to use a string and lay them to the line.

When the pattern reaches the border, bricks have to be cut and fitted into place. They should be tapped securely into base with handle of brick hammer.

To fill the cracks in the paving, sand was swept across the floor of the patio.

The finished patio with furniture in place, awaiting a Sunday afternoon family cookout.

position. Every so often, the bricks were aligned with a straight 2×4.

A better way to align the bricks is to stretch a string across the patio, as shown in the photo. Lay the brick to the line, but just short of it. The string need not be used to align every course; it can be moved three courses each time and the bricks laid to meet it.

As the work progresses, add more sand as needed and tamp well. If the job is moving along, tamping will keep one person busy most of the time. Another can be assigned the job of keeping bricks stacked in the work area.

The bricks should be laid to the border, the cut filler bricks put in last. It is very time consuming and interferes with the work to cut every piece as it runs against the border.

The filler bricks are cut in the shape of a right triangle with the acute angles approximately 45 degrees. Wear gloves when cutting them. Use a brick-set chisel and lay the brick on soft ground.

After all the bricks have been laid, throw a couple of shovels of sand on the surface and sweep it into the joints with a regular house broom. Sweep in different directions and the sand will easily fill all voids. You can add a little portland cement (1 to 6 ratio), which stiffens the sand and prevents it from washing out of the joints.

Now you can enjoy the fruits of all that hard work. Put the patio furniture in place, mix a cooling drink, and relax in a comfortable chair. Then christen the patio with a cookout for everyone who helped you do the job.

Plastic grid (below) can be used as a guide for laying bricks in a basketweave bond. Note screed board in foreground for leveling sand.

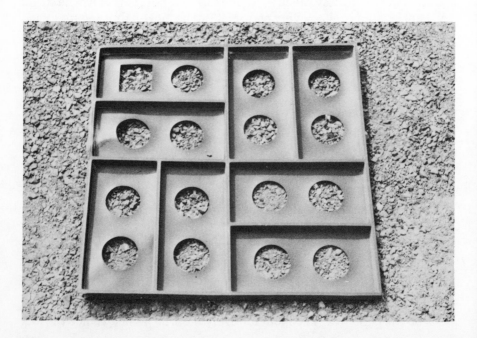

Paving with plastic grids. A cleverly made plastic frame for laying brick in basketweave or herringbone bond is available at many building-supply dealers. The frame will hold eight modular (3⅝″ × 7⅝″) bricks in perfect alignment. It works like this: Once the sand and stone dust are in place, you lay the plastic frames next to each other on the bed. Then the bricks are laid in the frame. After all the bricks are laid, sand is swept into the joints. The frames are worth the extra expense, as they save time and produce a neat job.

Another method of laying brick pavings is with the aid of a grid made of treated 2×4s. The bricks are laid, in a running bond, within the grid, as shown in the accompanying photo.

Brick paving laid in an adaptation of a running bond between treated 2×4s.

12 | Building Steps of Brick

The purpose of any flight of steps is to allow people to move from one level to another with a minimum of effort. In addition to their functional value, steps can also form an attractive part of your home or garden. Concrete steps are the standard type usually found on most houses, but they add little in the way of character or style. Brick or stone, on the other hand, blend with other architectural features and lend themselves to more interesting designs.

There is no set rule that steps have to be built in a straight line. They can curve or wind and be interrupted by landings. But the principles of step building, with respect to proportions and design, are always the same.

Typical step construction, showing dimensions of various components and their relationship.

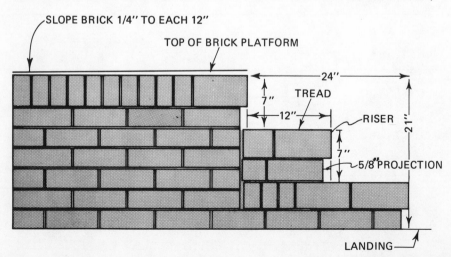

There are certain terms used in step construction that are helpful to know. The first part of the step, on which you place your foot when ascending or descending, is known as the *tread.* The vertical part between two treads is the *riser.* The part of the porch that adjoins the first step at the top is called the *platform.* The base at the bottom is called the *landing.*

The relationship between the tread and riser is important, not only for appearance, but for safety and comfort. The risers should be an easy lift for the leg; the treads should provide ample room for the foot. The risers and treads should be uniform throughout the stairway.

A good rule to follow is that twice the height of the riser plus the depth of the tread should be 25" to 27". Like all rules, it is flexible and can be bent to fit some situations. In general, though, a garden step should have 6" riser and a 15" tread. Steps leading to the front door generally have a 12" tread and a 7" riser.

Over the years the following dimensions have evolved that present the best combination of treads and risers for step construction.

Riser Height	Tread Width
4"	18"
5"	17"
6"	14"
7"	12"

The width of the steps is another consideration. Minimum width for garden steps should be no less than 4', which will accommodate two persons walking side by side. There are times when you will have to carry lawn furniture, benches, or other bulky items down the steps, so make them big enough. Garden steps have always been known for small risers and deep treads. Steps leading to a front door are usually about 3' wide. The platform at the top is normally larger, allowing plenty of room at the door.

If the stairway consists of a number of steps, and it will be used by young children or older people, it is wise to install handrails. In many areas of the country the building code requires them.

LAYING OUT STEPS.   There are two methods of laying brick steps. You can use a stretcher course with a header laid on top or a stretcher course with a rowlock course on top. I prefer to lay a rowlock on top as it provides a 7" rise, which is the best height. Each tread should slope slightly to allow for drainage. A ⅝" projection at the front of the tread prevents water from running down the riser below it.

You can easily figure how many steps are needed to climb any incline. First measure the height of the steps. In the illustration, the height from the bottom of the porch to the top is 21". Dividing this figure by 7" (height of rise) gives us exactly three risers. Since the last riser is taken from the top of the last step to the platform, only two treads are needed. As the tread measures 12″ deep, we would start the first step 24″ (2″ × 12″) from the porch. Remember that the rowlock brick on top of the tread projects about ⅝″ to form a drop; allow for this when laying the first course. The top of the platform would have a slope of approximately ¼″ to the foot to drain water away from the door.

Two methods of laying brick steps: a stretcher course with rowlock on top (top drawing); a stretcher course with header on top (bottom). Walkways can be laid in basketweave pattern (top) or in a running bond (bottom). *Courtesy Brick Institute.*

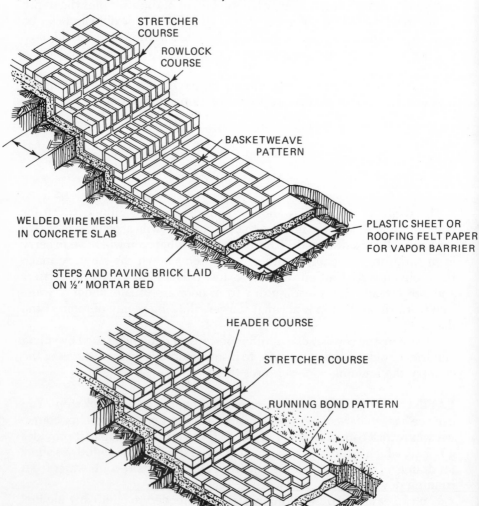

STRETCHER COURSE

ROWLOCK COURSE

BASKETWEAVE PATTERN

WELDED WIRE MESH IN CONCRETE SLAB

PLASTIC SHEET OR ROOFING FELT PAPER FOR VAPOR BARRIER

STEPS AND PAVING BRICK LAID ON ½″ MORTAR BED

HEADER COURSE

STRETCHER COURSE

RUNNING BOND PATTERN

BRICK-FACING CONCRETE STEPS. A friend of mine had a concrete porch and steps in front of his house that, over the years, had settled and cracked. We decided to rebuild the steps and porch by laying brick over the concrete. Had we started from scratch, we would have poured the steps and porch in forms, allowed the concrete to dry, and then faced it with brick. But since the concrete steps were still in good enough condition to serve as a foundation for a brick facing, we could eliminate the first step. The following photos show the procedure of building a brick facing on a concrete porch and steps.

1. Concrete porch and steps that were given a brick facelift. We dug 6″ excavation, 12″ wide, for footing around porch and steps. Then we poured concrete.

2. After concrete had set for a day, I plumbed with a level from edge of porch to footing, and marked footing in several places.

3. Using old bricks for the first courses below grade, I built wall to enclose concrete porch and steps. I filled space between brickwork and wall with mortar.

4. Brickwork was built up level with top of first step. Rowlock course would be laid next.

5. I laid rowlock bricks on ends of steps, then continued building wall to porch height.

6. Porch wall was completed and a few rowlocks on each end of the steps were laid and allowed to set, to prevent center bricks from pushing outward.

7. Stretching a line along the front of the rowlock course to align the bricks.

8. To keep rowlock course even, I used a long level and tapped bricks into position.

9. Measuring with a modular rule, I check to be sure I can complete course without cutting brick. Rule reads No. 6, allowing for last head joint.

10. After steps were completed, I laid a header course around the porch. This served as a border for laying bricks across the entire porch.

11. The completed porch and steps. The surrounding soil was graded, shrubbery planted and enclosed with a brick border.

13 | Building a Single-Flue Brick Chimney

In recent years there has been a tremendous increase in building fireplaces and chimneys, due mostly to the high cost of energy and heating a home. Building a chimney is not beyond the ability of the handyman, but it is important to understand the principles and rules of construction before starting. Safety is also a prime consideration because you are working with fire and heat.

A single-flue chimney, which we will be concerned with in this chapter, will service one fireplace, wood stove, or oil-burner furnace. A flue can handle only one heat source because the air currents in the chimney would otherwise conflict with each other, causing the heating device to emit smoke into the room.

PLANNING. After deciding where the chimney is to be built and what type of heating device you want, you will have to obtain a permit from your local building-permits office. There is usually a small charge. The permits office will point out local and national building and fire-code requirements. These are practical and should be no problem. Generally, there are a couple of helpful folders available for the asking. Jot down any questions you have before going so you won't overlook anything. Good relations with the building inspector save a lot of headaches later on. As the job progresses, he will make periodic inspection trips to give you the go-ahead for the next phase of construction.

MATERIALS FOR THE CHIMNEY. The traditional chimney is made of brick, but chimneys can also be made of concrete block or stone. Concrete chimney blocks are available in different sizes according to the flue lining that will be inside them. A special chimney block is also made with a rounded hole to allow installation of the fireproof connector that goes from the stovepipe into the chimney. One advantage of using chimney

Concrete blocks for building chimney come in different sizes.

block is that it does not take long to build. Stone, on the other hand, takes a lot more time and work.

If you plan to use bricks, select good hard bricks, preferably with no holes. Choose a color that complements your home; if your home is made of bricks, match the chimney bricks as closely as possible. (The photographs in this chapter show a brick chimney I built on an existing house for a family who wanted to install a wood-burning stove.)

Flue linings. To prolong its life, a chimney should be lined with a burned clay-tile flue lining. In most areas of the country a flue lining is required by the building code. Most chimneys use rectangular flue linings for bricks or masonry, although they are available in circular shapes as well. They come in 2′ lengths that are set in mortar on top of each other as the chimney is built.

Burned-clay flue linings are available to fit rectangular or round chimney interiors.

Fireproof connector. The connector, also called a flue ring or thimble, passes through the house wall into the chimney. The stovepipe is inserted into it. The thimble is available in different diameters and lengths. It is made of burned fire clay, the same as the flue lining. Be careful when handling either because they will break easily if dropped or banged around.

Mortar and footing. You will need a supply of building sand for the footing and the mortar for laying the bricks. Mortar for a chimney can be standard masonry cement, or you can mix portland cement, lime, and sand. I recommend masonry cement because you only have to add sand and water. It saves time and is less trouble to mix. A good selection for chimney mortar is Type S, which is a little stronger than Type N. Type N is average but will also do the job.

The footing mix is 1 part portland cement to 2 parts sand to 3 parts crushed stone. Just remember the 1-2-3 ratio.

Clean-out door. A metal clean-out door is built into the chimney for removal of soot or ashes. It is a must. Insist on a cast-iron door from your building-supply dealer. It costs a few dollars more, but will last longer without rusting out and is worth the difference in price.

Nails and wall ties. You'll need a supply of 10d nails and wall ties for tying the brickwork to the existing building if the house is of frame construction. If it is made of bricks, you can still use the wall ties but will need a tempered nail to drive in the old mortar joints.

You can't start the chimney or order the bricks until a decision is made on the size of the chimney. How big it will be depends on how big the flue lining is that it will enclose. In turn, the flue-lining size is determined by the draft requirements of the heating device—in this case, the wood stove.

The solution is simple, if you remember this rule: For a good draft, a flue lining's cross-sectional area should always be at least 25 percent greater

Brick layout for a single-flue chimney. To accommodate expansion, a minimum of 1″ of air space should be left around lining.

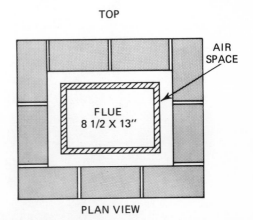

TOP

AIR SPACE

FLUE
8 1/2 X 13″

PLAN VIEW

than the connector's or stovepipe's. A wood stove with an outlet 8″ in diameter, for example, has a cross-sectional area of 64″—8″ × 8″ equals 64″. The closest practical flue size would be 8½″ × 13″ (outside dimensions). The thickness of the flue-lining walls is so small (½″) that it is not taken into account. Multiplying 8½″ by 13″ yields 110.5″, easily 25 percent more than the 64″ figured for the stovepipe. A flue lining that is too small will restrict the draft; one that is too large will pull too much of the heat up the chimney.

Once you know what flue-lining size to use, you can determine the layout of the brickwork. A flue lining should not be walled around solidly because the expansion of the chimney when it is hot tends to crack the brickwork. Leave at least 1″ space around the flue. This allows for expansion as well as for any differences in brick length. Bricks are a little larger than 8″ due to the burning in the kiln.

FOOTING AND FOUNDATION.   When excavating for the footing, be sure of two important points: (1) it must be below the frost line, and (2) it should rest on undisturbed soil. The building inspector will check these two requirements when he visits. Dig the hole for the chimney approximately 24″ longer and wider than is actually needed for the size of the chimney. This will spread the concentrated weight of the chimney over

Excavation for chimney footing should be dug below frost line. Steel rods are laid in the bottom of hole for extra strength.

a larger area. The allowance for footing depth should be at least 12″ due to the weight. Don't fudge on the footing.

After cleaning out all the earth, lay some reinforcement in the bottom of the hole. Steel rods, concrete wire, or some lengths of old pipe will do. Contact the building inspector, who will examine the excavation before any concrete is poured. This is one of the critical requirements for the permit approval. After approval of the inspector, mix the concrete in a ratio of 1 part portland cement, 2 parts sand, and 3 parts stone or gravel, and pour it into the hole. Let it cure for a day or so before going any farther.

Concrete for footing is mixed in mortar box, carried to chimney site in wheelbarrow.

Pouring the concrete for footing into excavation.

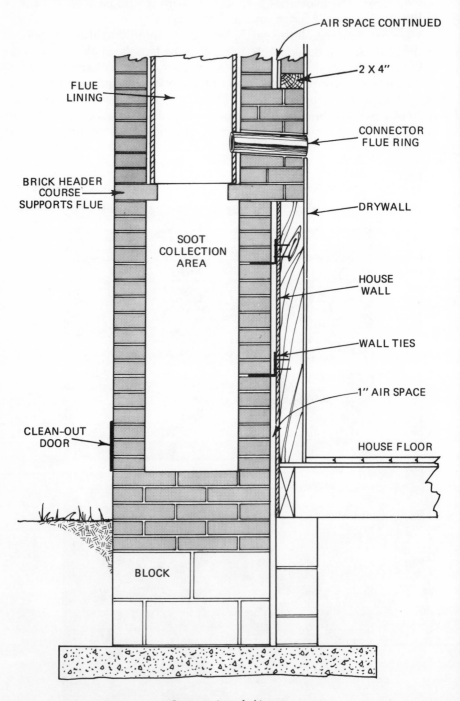

AIR SPACE CONTINUED

2 X 4"

CONNECTOR FLUE RING

FLUE LINING

DRYWALL

BRICK HEADER COURSE SUPPORTS FLUE

SOOT COLLECTION AREA

HOUSE WALL

WALL TIES

1" AIR SPACE

CLEAN-OUT DOOR

HOUSE FLOOR

BLOCK

Cross section of chimney.

For the foundation, lay concrete blocks or bricks almost to the grade line of the chimney. If there are some old bricks or concrete blocks around the place, these will be fine for the foundation. Stop your masonry work about 6″ below the grade line so the old bricks or blocks will not show if the chimney eventually settles. Fill in the center of the chimney with masonry scraps and mortar until the height of the clean-out door is reached.

INSTALLING THE CLEAN-OUT DOOR. Build the door into the brickwork where it will be easy to get to when removing soot. The best method is to build the jambs for the opening of brick up to the height of the door. Smooth the mortar in the bottom of the interior of the chimney where the door will be situated.

The clean-out door has a top and bottom; examine the hinges to see which way it sits. Spread a bed of mortar on the brick on which it will sit and butter a good mortar joint on each side of the opening. Set the door in place and press mortar on the inside around the door. Some doors have small holes in the metal frame on the sides where a nail can be inserted through the metal into the mortar joint. This helps to hold the door in place. Prop the door with a stick so that it stays in place until you are finished.

Bridge over the door with your brickwork and prop up with a piece of

This photo shows brickwork completed to the grade line. An opening has been left in one side for a clean-out door.	Installing clean-out door in opening. Door is held in place with mortar. Some doors have holes in frame for nailing into mortar joint.

wood and some unmortared bricks, which are removed after the brick-work has set. Then build the brickwork up to scaffold height. The Building Officials and Code Administrators International Inc. (BOCA) requires that when a chimney is built against a frame house (which this one was) the brickwork should be a minimum of 1″ away from the house. Later this space is filled with a noncombustible material.

FLUE-LINING AND THIMBLE INSTALLATION. The first flue lining should be set in the chimney about 8″ lower than the bottom of the flue ring. It must sit securely on the brickwork. This is accomplished by laying a header-brick course at this level and letting the header brick project into the chimney far enough for the flue to sit on. You will have to cut off the brick header to the length desired as a full header brick would be too long.

Before the flue ring can be built into the flue a round hole must be cut through the flue lining to receive it. First, check the flue lining to make sure it does not have a crack in it. Tap lightly with the hammer; if it is cracked it will emit a dead, flat sound. If so, get another one. Using the flue ring as a pattern, draw an outline on the flue where the hole is to be cut. The burned-clay lining is hard and brittle, and the only safe way to cut the hole is to pack the flue with sand first, tamping tightly. The sand will support the walls of the flue and prevent it from breaking, *if* you take it easy when you cut.

Chimney is now at scaffold height, the top of the house's brick foundation. One inch of air space must be left between chimney and house wall.

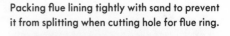
Packing flue lining tightly with sand to prevent it from splitting when cutting hole for flue ring.

After chipping hole in center of circle with point chisel, I carefully chip away opening for flue ring.

View inside house showing installation of flue ring in brickwork. Opening in wall will be repaired with fireproof material.

Chip a hole directly in the center of the circle with a point chisel, working gently. Then gradually chip away until you reach the edges of the circle which you have marked on the flue lining. Cut the hole just a little bigger than the pencil mark to allow for a mortar joint when setting the flue ring. If you don't rush, you should have no trouble.

After the hole has been cut, set the flue lining in the chimney on the header course, in mortar. Where the flue ring passes through the wall to reach the chimney flue, brickwork should be laid for fireproofing. No less than 6″ of brickwork should be built around the flue ring. In a frame house such as this one, you will have to nail a 2×4 between the studs below the flue ring and build up the brickwork on it. Be sure there are no electrical wires in the immediate area inside the wall.

When the bricks have reached the proper height, mortar the flue ring into the chimney flue. The flue ring must extend through the masonry wall to the inner face of the flue liner and not beyond, and be cemented in fully. This will make a good fireproof connection. (The flue ring should pitch slightly toward the stove—¼″ to the foot.)

Chimney is now midway up side of house. Gin pole attached to scaffolding allows materials to be raised with rope and pulley.

Chimney should be built at least 24" above and 10' from peak of roof.

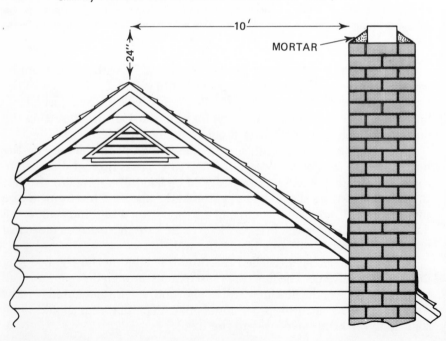

COMPLETING THE CHIMNEY. Erect a scaffold as needed to build the chimney up to the roof. Metal scaffolding can be rented inexpensively and is a lot safer than wood. You can simplify lifting materials up to the scaffold by hooking up a rope and pulley on a metal pole, which you can build from pipe or rent.

If the roof overhangs the walls of the house, it will be necessary to cut a hole for the chimney to pass through. Unless you have the necessary skills, I recommend that you get a carpenter for this job because it's easy to damage the roof. Since the chimney is built *through* the roof, metal flashing will have to be installed around the chimney and fitted under the shingles to prevent water leakage. This is also a job for a carpenter. In instances like these, it's wiser to spend the extra money now than be sorry later.

Most building codes specify that the top of the chimney be at least 2′ above the roof if the distance from the peak of the roof to the chimney is under 10′. This will prevent downdrafts and cause the chimney to work more efficiently. If the chimney is more than 10′ away from the peak of the roof, the height of the chimney could be less than 2′ above the roof. However, it is best to check this with your local building inspector.

THE DRAFT. The draft (air current in the chimney that carries away hot gases and smoke) should be strong enough to exert a good pull if it is going to do the job. You can check this with a simple test: Roll a piece of paper into a tube, light it with a match, and hold it near the flue ring in the chimney. The draft, if it is working properly, should pull the flame and

Check draft in chimney with rolled-up newspaper. Note how draft pulls flame into flue.

Wood stove was installed on brick hearth, in front of fireproof wall. Metal hood traps heat and moves it through existing duct system in the house. This stove replaced forced-air system and heated entire house.

smoke up the chimney. If not, make sure there are no obstructions in the flue and that the chimney has been built up to the correct height.

Even if the chimney is built perfectly and the stove installed correctly, there has to be ample fresh air entering the room for good combustion to occur. This is the problem with many electrically heated homes with fireplaces. The house is sealed so tightly that no air can enter. If your stove does not burn properly and smokes, try opening a window a crack and see if this makes any difference. Also, for safety's sake, when installing your wood stove, be sure to set it on noncombustible material, such as concrete, bricks, or asbestos.

Remember: The importance of good workmanship cannot be stressed enough when building a chimney. Since a chimney is a column, it will be very noticeable if it gets out of plumb. Take your time and strive for accuracy in laying the bricks.

14 | Building a Heat-Circulating Fireplace and Chimney

This is one of the more demanding masonry projects a homeowner or handyman can undertake. You are going to have to do a little studying beforehand and, in the building of a one-flue chimney, observe the rules of recommended construction. It will result in big savings because the average fireplace and chimney cost somewhere around $3,500 to $4,000 if built by a professional mason or contractor. That should give you a little incentive.

The advantages of having a fireplace in your home are threefold: (1) it will definitely cut down those expensive heating costs; (2) it will give you an emergency source of heat if the power goes off; and (3) it will increase the value of your home. In the long run, it will be a very profitable investment.

You will, of course, have to get a building permit for the job. The permits office will probably want to see a rough sketch of the project, so after reading this chapter and other reference materials, draw one and take it along.

BASIC CONSTRUCTION PRINCIPLES. It will help in the beginning to get a picture in your mind of how a standard masonry fireplace and chimney are built. Examining the cross section of a typical masonry fireplace and chimney from top to bottom, you can see that it will require a good footing—a foundation which may or may not have an ash pit, based on the preference of the builder. If no ash pit is built in the chimney foundation, the ashes are taken out of the inner hearth. A clean-out door will be needed if an ash pit is included.

The hearth is composed of two areas, an inner firebrick hearth with an ash-dump door (if the ash pit is desired), and an outer hearth made of bricks or tiles. The hearth base is constructed of reinforced concrete and tied into the chimney for strength. The firebox area is built of firebrick and has a metal damper at the top to regulate the draft. A brick smoke shelf

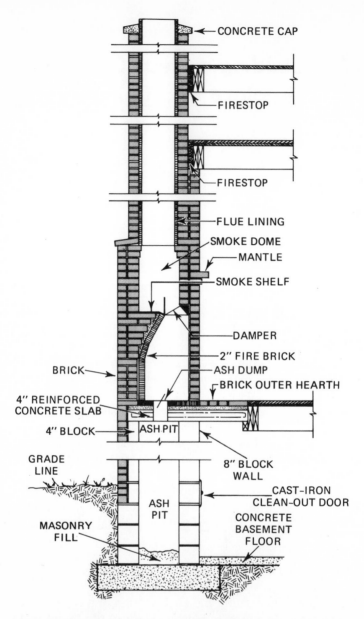

CONCRETE CAP

FIRESTOP

FIRESTOP

FLUE LINING
SMOKE DOME
MANTLE
SMOKE SHELF

DAMPER
2" FIRE BRICK
BRICK
ASH DUMP
BRICK OUTER HEARTH
4" REINFORCED CONCRETE SLAB
4" BLOCK
ASH PIT
GRADE LINE
8" BLOCK WALL
CAST-IRON CLEAN-OUT DOOR
ASH PIT
CONCRETE BASEMENT FLOOR
MASONRY FILL

Cross section of a typical chimney and heat-circulating fireplace.

in back of the damper deflects the draft which comes down and sends it back up the chimney. At the same time, air is drawn into the fireplace through the opening to complete the draft cycle.

The area from the top of the damper to the first flue liner is the smoke dome, or chamber. The flue lining rests on bricks which have been racked out (corbeled) to create a smooth, inclined passageway from the damper to the top of the smoke dome. This promotes a smooth draft.

The flue lining is enclosed by brickwork, a minimum of 4", or one thickness of brick, to the top of the chimney. The top of the flue should extend 6" above the top of the brickwork with a mortar wash or cap. The top of the chimney has to be a minimum of 2' above the peak of the roof to prevent downdrafts. Where the chimney passes woodwork on the interior of the house, a minimum clearance of 2" is recommended, and this area should be filled with fireproof material. This is basically how any chimney with a fireplace is constructed whether a circulator unit is used or not.

THE CIRCULATOR FIREPLACE. A conventional masonry fireplace as just described is a very inadequate heating system because the majority of heat goes up the chimney. At the price of firewood, which is pushing $100 a cord, you will want to retain as much of that heat as possible. A conventional masonry fireplace gives off heat by radiation, which is in a straight line, much like the rays of the sun when they strike an object. A metal circulating fireplace, however, works on the principles of convection, much like a forced-air furnace. It forces the heated air throughout the room or house.

There are a number of metal circulator fireplace units that can be obtained from your local building-supply dealer. One I like and have used several times is the VestalAire Circulator Fireplace. This fireplace unit is built of heavy-gauge steel and the firebox area of $3/16$" boiler plate. The secret of its success is that its walls are hollow chambers a couple of inches

Metal circulator fireplace unit is one-piece shell, ready to set on the hearth.

HIGH SMOKE DOME

VESTALAIRE

FULL-SIZE SMOKE SHELF 3/16" BOILERPLATE

CLOSE-FITTING DAMPER

SQUARE CORNERS ELIMINATE DIAGONAL BRICK COURSES

FULL-SIZE THROAT OPENING

WARM AIR OUTLET

ONE-PIECE FIREBOX 3 16" BOILERPLATE

HEATING CHAMBER FOR CIRCULATING AIR

BAFFLE PLATE

GLASS WOOL INSULATION

EASILY CONTROLLED DAMPER HANDLE

COOL AIR INLET

Metal fireplace units on display in showroom of a building-supply dealer. Unit at right has an open back.

apart. As unheated air enters through the grille near the bottom of the fireplace it is heated by the hot inner wall, rises through the space, and is forced back into the room through another set of grilles above the firebox area. Special fans for the unit can be installed in the cool-air inlet of the grille frame to pull air through faster, making the fireplace even more efficient.

The unit also includes a throat, a high smoke dome over the firebox area, and a built-in damper. It is funnel-shaped at the top to fit the flue lining set on corbeled bricks directly above the opening. Enough insulation comes with the unit to completely enclose it. This prevents heat loss and allows room for expansion (no masonry should touch the metal unit).

The metal circulator fireplace is scientifically designed and built at the factory to the correct proportions for efficient operation, so there is not much of a chance that you will foul up. It eliminates the know-how of building the most difficult areas of the fireplace. If I seem biased, it's true —all things considered, the savings in the installation, plus the increased heat output and the efficiency of design, make it the ideal choice for a new fireplace in this day of high energy costs.

Size and cost.   Generally the size of a fireplace is determined by the room size. A standard basis for working this out, published by the U.S. Department of Agriculture, states: "A fireplace 30"–36" wide is generally suitable for a room having 300 square feet of floor. The width should be increased for larger rooms. . . ."

The VestalAire Circulator Fireplace is available in widths from 28" to 48", so you can use this as a guide. It is difficult to quote costs the way prices are rising, but at this time it is safe to figure on $300 for the unit, including delivery to your home. If you are thinking of getting one, it is a good idea to order as soon as possible; the demand has been very great and you may have to wait.

CONSTRUCTION DETAILS.   It's impossible to cover all of the specific installation details here due to the individual nature of each job. Most companies supply them with the unit, though. The circulator featured in the photographs in this chapter was an add-on to an existing house, which required opening the wall for access. When constructing a new home, this type of problem would not crop up because the unit can be incorporated in the original building plans. However, the construction procedures are basically the same. Since most circulating fireplaces installed by the homeowner will probably be add-ons, I selected this type of installation to demonstrate here.

The add-on fireplace requires the cutting of an opening through the wall to hook up the fireplace to the chimney. Special care will have to be taken to keep all furniture covered up or moved out of the way.

Pouring the footing.   The first job is to excavate the area for the footing by digging down to undisturbed soil. The soil around this house was almost all fill dirt so we had to dig all of the way to the footing level of the house. Since a lot of excavating was involved, it was necessary to get a backhoe to do the work.

Code requirements will be different in some areas, but generally if you make the footing 12″ deep and about 18″ wider than the chimney on all sides, it will support the load. Steel reinforcement rods, lengths of steel pipe or concrete reinforcement wire should be laid in the bottom of the hole for extra strength. It is not uncommon for a chimney with a fireplace to weigh more than 8 tons, concentrated in a small area.

The concrete is poured as a pad, and if you give the size to the dispatcher at the concrete company, he can figure what you will need very accurately. If you need a cubic yard or more of concrete, spend the money and get it delivered by truck, premixed. Mixing this much concrete yourself is a tough job and not worth the trouble.

After the concrete is placed, let it cure for at least two days before attempting to work on it. It will cure better if you dampen it with a hose periodically. This prevents surface cracking.

Laying the foundation.   You can build the foundation with various sizes of concrete blocks. The most practical size to handle is the 8″ block. You'll need a good number of blocks because the foundation has to be solid. A trip to the closest block plant can save some money here. Many times a plant will offer "seconds," blocks that are a little twisted, chipped, off-size, or have some other minor defect. While they would not be suitable for a finished job that is seen, they are excellent for the foundation of a chimney,

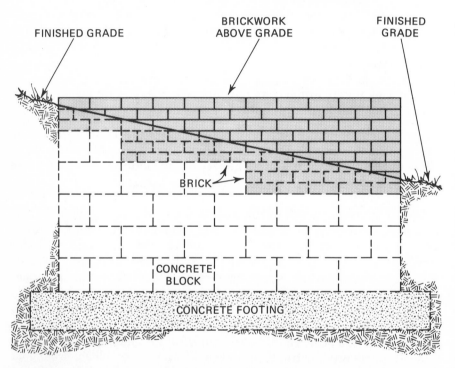

Block foundation for chimney was built to grade line, where brickwork starts (top). Hole in wall is for installing a flue ring for wood stove. Section view is shown in drawing.

and are usually about half the price of new blocks. It is certainly worth checking out if you need a lot of blocks, although you will probably have to pick them up at the plant and transport them yourself.

Before laying out any blocks on the footing, mark off on the exterior wall of the house where the chimney will be after it has been built up to grade level. Then plumb down with a level and mark with a pencil or crayon where it will be on the footing. Brush the footing off and spread a full bed of mortar for the first course of block. On this particular job, since the earth was already excavated, we thought it would be a good idea to cut a hole through the basement wall and insert a flue ring for a future wood stove hook-up to heat the basement. The flue lining for the wood stove could be built in the side of the chimney without interfering with the fireplace on the first floor since there was plenty of space for the added flue. After this was worked out, the foundation was then built up to the grade level where the brickwork would start.

The brickwork.   The brick was laid on the lowest end of the chimney and stepped up to meet the next course of block. This coincided with the grade of the earth at this point. A clean-out door was built into the end wall of the chimney so soot could be removed from the wood-stove flue when necessary. The brickwork was then built up to the level of the interior floor of the house where an opening had to be cut through the wall to accommodate the installation of the metal fireplace unit.

As soon as the brickwork has hardened, it is a good practice to fill in around the foundation to make work easier and to prevent anyone from falling into the opening and injuring himself. This is especially true if young children are around.

After installing flue ring, author builds clean-out door into brickwork for wood-stove hook-up.

Opening the wall. Before making any cuts, check if there are any electrical outlets or wires in the wall which may be in the way. If so, and you are not knowledgeable about electricity, call an electrician to remove them. This is a job you either do or do not know about and you can't take any chances. The same is true if you have second thoughts about damaging the house by cutting through it. If you understand framing, though, it is simply a matter of cutting out the opening and strengthening it as you go.

To cut an opening through a wood-frame wall, mark off the area to be cut out (this allows for the metal circulating fireplace and space for the brickwork that will go around it). Then drill a hole at each corner of the area and strike a chalk line around the border. Start with a keyhole saw (a long, tapered saw) in the bored hole and saw until there is enough room to insert a carpenter's cross-cut saw, which will be faster. I would stay away from using a power saw because you could hit a nail or it could kick back.

Opening must be cut in house wall for fireplace. When wall framing has been cut, 2×4 jack studs and 2×6 header are installed to support load.

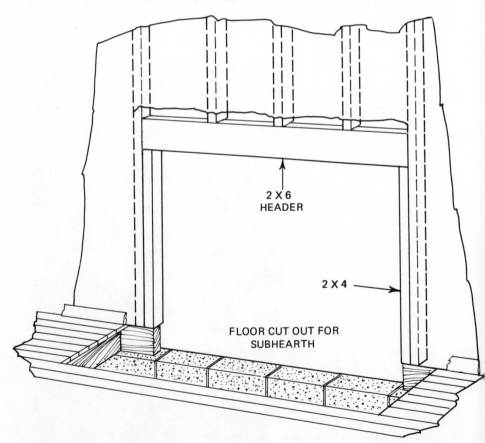

2 X 6
HEADER

2 X 4

FLOOR CUT OUT FOR
SUBHEARTH

Opening has been cut in brick wall to accommodate add-on fireplace. Before cutting through wall, be sure to check for electric outlets or wires.

Finding the studs is no problem: look where the nails are lined up vertically. Cut out and around all of the studs first, removing all of the sheathing materials, insulation, etc.

Remember, the studs are supporting the weight of the wall and roof. This load will have to be supported by other bracing such as 2×4s or 2×6s. A wood header can be fitted in place to span the opening, rests on jack studs on each side.

If your house is brick instead of frame the brick wall will have to be cut first and then the inside framing. A brick wall will carry its own weight without any bracing, if the hole is not too large, because of the bonding of the brickwork.

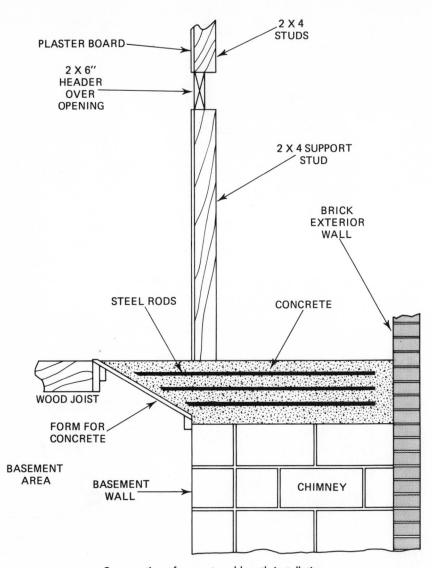

PLASTER BOARD

2 X 4 STUDS

2 X 6" HEADER OVER OPENING

2 X 4 SUPPORT STUD

BRICK EXTERIOR WALL

STEEL RODS

CONCRETE

WOOD JOIST

FORM FOR CONCRETE

BASEMENT AREA

BASEMENT WALL

CHIMNEY

Cross section of concrete subhearth installation.

Forming and pouring the subhearth. Before any bricks can be laid to set the metal unit on, a subhearth reinforced with steel rods will have to be installed. The floor should be cut out in front of the fireplace the length of the fireplace and 16" wide. This is standard for an outer hearth. A wood form is nailed to the joists to support the concrete. Steel rods are placed from the chimney into the formed area and the concrete is then poured. This will make a strong hearth because it is all joined together.

Laying the firebrick hearth. The fireplace form sits on a firebrick hearth. Hearths can be raised for appearance or be flush with the floor. There has

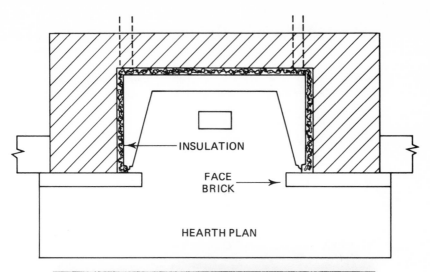

INSULATION

FACE
BRICK

HEARTH PLAN

Firebrick hearth completed, ready for metal circulator unit. Rough brick around edges will not show after unit is in position.

been a trend toward raised hearths in recent years. If the inner hearth is raised, the opening has to be higher to accommodate the unit. In the photo opposite a typical raised firebrick hearth is shown ready to receive a fireplace. Plastic in the background was put up to enclose the opening as it was raining at the time.

Bricking in the unit. When you set the metal unit on the hearth, get plenty of help; it's heavy. Position it so it is centered on the hearth and in line with the face of the interior wall. The brick facing will be gauged from the finished interior wall later.

Circulator unit in position. String across opening was used to hold insulation in place and now can be removed. Holes on each side of fireplace are for grilles, which will be built in when facing work is done.

Enough insulation should have come with the unit to encase it completely on the outside surface. There are different methods of wrapping the insulation around the unit. The simplest, I've found, is to have someone help and tie lengths of string around it. This holds the insulation in place until all of the masonry is done and it will stay there on its own. When all of the rough brickwork is done, you just cut the string off. It is important, however, that no brick or mortar touch the unit at any place, to allow for expansion.

Build up the rough bricks enclosing the unit. When you reach the area where the duct openings to the inner wall of the metal shell will be, leave openings, making sure they are no smaller than the holes in the metal units. You can smooth some mortar on the inside to make a good job in the duct area of your brickwork.

After about every five courses of bricks, lay some metal wall ties in the mortar joints and let them protrude to tie the facing bricks, which will be laid last. When the height of the hot-air grille is reached, build that duct in the same manner as the one below.

Build up to where enough space is present that a steel angle iron can be laid across the brick piers. The metal form will be slanting back on an angle at this point so the iron will clear it when the right height is reached. The angle iron is set in position and bricked across. It is a lot easier from now on to spot a brick on each end of the masonry work and attach a line to keep the brickwork straight. Add more wall ties as needed.

To finish off the rough installation, fill in with mortar all the way around the opening, using a pointing trowel. (I am assuming that the carpet and furniture have been covered and protected while all of this work is being done. The drop cloths or coverings can be gathered up and the dirt removed easily this way.)

Building the chimney to the roof overhang. With the inside work finished for the time being, scaffolding is erected and the chimney is built up to the roof overhang. The photograph shows what the chimney looked like when we resumed work outside. Notice that the insulation is all the way around the chimney, and you can see where the bottom ducts were built in with bricks. The top ducts will be built in the same way when that level is reached. Also, the rest of the insulation near the tapered top part of the shell will be put on as the work progresses.

A rope and pulley were attached to the frame of the scaffolding to transport materials from the ground. We also tied the scaffolding to the house with a length of rope to steady it; pulling materials up tends to shake it. It is a good idea to tie a guard rail across the edge of the scaffolding in case you slip. Make the work area as safe as possible.

Exterior view of chimney and fireplace after rough interior facing was completed. Additional insulation will be added as the chimney is built

Roof overhang was cut to admit chimney and flashing installed. Rubber underlayment on roof protects shingles and provides safe footing.

When we reached the roof overhang, we cut a hole for the chimney. It's important to cut the opening as neatly as possible because this area will have to be flashed to keep the water from entering the house or dripping down through the overhang.

The roof should be protected with some covering until the work is completed. I've found that rubber underlayment that is used for carpet is excellent because it is soft and will give. Sheets of tarpaper and some scraps of plywood also do a good job. You must be very careful, though, that the shingles or roofing are not damaged while you are working on the roof.

The flashing is built into the brickwork and fitted under the shingles to keep any water out. If you don't know how to flash, get help from someone who does. If this very important job is not done right, the roof will leak —a risk you can't afford to take.

COMPLETING THE FIREPLACE.   Start the facing of the fireplace by drybonding the bricks from one end to the other. Try to space them so full bricks can be used across the angle iron at the top of the opening. After the bond has been established, lay out each of the two piers on either side of the opening. Remember: the end of the piers should be slightly past the edge of the metal unit to hide the insulation near the edges.

Build the brick piers, mortaring in fully the grille frames in the holes you left when building in the metal shell. If fans are to be installed in the cool-air vents, now is the time to have the electrician run the wires. The wire going from them to the panel box can be hidden behind the brick facing, but it *has to be put in now.*

Laying bricks to the line at front of fireplace.

When the height of the firebox is reached, lay the steel angle iron on the piers and continue building the brickwork. The hot-air grille is also built into the proper space, a little above the top of the firebox. Make sure the grilles are plumb and level when walled in or the cover will look lopsided when it is put on.

As when building in the rough work, spot a brick on each end of the fireplace and attach a line for laying bricks. It will keep the wall straight. Build wall ties into the bed joints of the new work so all the masonry will be tied together. They were left projecting out of the rough masonry and are flexible enough that if the new work does not come out evenly with the old they can be used by bending them to fit into the mortar joint.

Use a modular rule to mark off the courses of bricks from the ceiling down to make sure that full courses will work out. The time to check this is when you are about where the angle iron is set over the opening.

Laying the hearth. When the fireplace is completed, lay the hearth. The fireplace shown here has a one-piece stone hearth that spans its entire length. You can use bricks, tiles, or flagstone for hearths. The stones used for this fireplace blended in very well with the brickwork. The addition of a fire screen or glass fire doors will contain the sparks and finish the job.

The completed fireplace.

15 | Repointing Brickwork

An old brick home can be made to look like new by cutting out and repointing the old mortar joints with new mortar. Repointing will, in all probability, also require cutting out and replacing soft bricks that have deteriorated. This is especially true in very old buildings.

There are two basic reasons for repointing brick masonry: (1) to make the wall watertight, and (2) to restore the brickwork to its original condition. If the joints in a wall are bad and not repaired, they can only get worse, which will eventually cost you a lot of money.

Most of the repointing that a homeowner will want to do is fairly simple. If an historic building is being repointed, the mortar has to be analyzed and matched for color. Your only concern is that the mortar color be about the same throughout and that the mortar bonds to the old bricks. Leave the historic work to the professionals.

Repointing a brick wall is not a job that can be rushed. It is also mostly all handwork since the mortar joints should be cut out with a chisel; power grinders can ruin the edges of the bricks.

Mortar for repointing is different from mortar used in regular masonry work. The primary task in repointing is to establish a good bond between bricks and mortar. The compressive strength of the mortar is less important. Older bricks, as a rule, are softer than new ones, and the mortar joints that you will be cutting out will also be softer. It does no good to repoint a rich, new mortar against a soft, old one—they will not knit together properly. It is a common mistake to believe that the harder the mortar is, the better. A softer mortar will stretch more and be more compatible with softer brick.

MORTAR FOR REPOINTING. Mortars with a high percentage of portland cement are very hard and brittle, making them subject to excessive shrinkage from the edges of old brick and to hairline cracking. I have found that a high-lime-content mortar is much better than masonry ce-

1. Using a joint chisel with a tapered blade, cut out the old mortar joints to a depth of ½" to 1", depending on the hardness of the mortar. Cut the joint square so the new mortar can fill it completely.

2. After the joint has been cut out, brush out old mortar and dust well. A regular wallpaper brush is good for this. Then wet the joints with water so the repointing mortar will not dry out too quickly. Don't soak joints, dampen them.

3. Check the depth of the joint with a rule to make sure it's deep enough. The 1" depth shown here would be typical of an old brick wall with soft mortar.

4. Point and tuck the new mortar firmly in the joints with a flat slicker tool. Get a slicker ¼" wide on one end, ½" on the other. As you point, you may have to rewet the joints as they dry out.

5. When the joints have set, brush the wall with a medium-soft brush.

ment for repointing work. A good mortar mix is 1 part portland cement, 2 parts hydrated lime, and 8 parts sand. Sand could be increased to 9 parts for very old, soft brick. Mortar with a higher lime content will be a lot more waterproof because it will bond better to the brick. Good mortar is the key to successful repointing.

To prepare pointing mortar, mix the ingredients according to the proportions suggested above, using only enough water to be able to press the mix into a damp ball. After letting it set for approximately one-half hour, add more water to make it workable for pointing. Called prehydrating the mortar, this helps to cut down on the shrinkage that normally occurs.

Don't mix big batches for repointing—the work will be too slow for that. Any mortar that has not been used in a period of two hours will start to lose its strength and should be discarded.

The mortar should be a little stiffer than regular brick mortar so it will be easy to work with when using the pointing tools. If your sand pile has any gravel or small rocks in it, run the sand through an old window screen or similar material to remove them. It is frustrating to point mortar that has grit or gravel in it. The same is true if your portland cement has been sitting around for a long time and has hard lumps in it. The materials for making repointing mortar are not that expensive, so always use good, fresh ingredients. Repointing mortar can be retempered or loosened up about two times if it gets stiff due to water loss from evaporation. After that, throw it away and mix a new batch.

I have found that pointing from top to bottom keeps the wall cleaner. And if scaffolding is being rented, this will turn it loose earlier. If you are going to cut out mortar joints one day and repoint the next day, flush out the joints with a garden hose that has a nozzle. This is excellent for removing dust and old mortar particles. To save the most time when repointing, concentrate on one area at a time. Don't jump around. When one wall is finished, clean it up and go on to the next.

Be especially careful of repointing brickwork in cold weather. The small amount of mortar pointed back into the joints could freeze quickly. If the temperature drops below 38° F, I would not recommend repointing.

If the weather is very hot and dry, as it is in the summer, you will have to redampen the wall after repointing to make sure the mortar cures slowly. Use a fine spray of water from a garden hose or a tank-type garden spray. However, be careful not to soak the wall; this could cause the joints to wash out or streak onto the brick face.

16 | Cleaning Brickwork

After your brickwork has been completed and has cured, it should be cleaned to bring out the color and remove all splatters of mortar. You should try to keep your masonry work as clean as possible when building the project, but it is inevitable that some mortar will be left on the wall when the job is finished.

Here are a few tips for keeping the work clean: (1) don't make the mortar so wet that it smears the brick; (2) cover the wall each time you finish working to prevent rain from splashing it; and (3) be especially careful that the wheelbarrow is not parked too close to the wall—mortar can splash out of it onto the work. The same is true for the mortar board.

Safety clothing. Masonry cleaners are liquid and tend to splash. Therefore, it's important to wear protective clothing. Protect your eyes with a pair of goggles. Protect your hands with rubber gloves, preferably the long-arm type. Wear rubber-coated or plastic pants. Since you'll be using water to rinse the wall, it's a good idea to wear a pair of rubber overshoes.

Cleaners. A number of different cleaners can be used for washing down brickwork. They are carried by the building-supply dealer under a variety of brand names and are known as "proprietary" cleaning compounds. The most popular and inexpensive old standby, which I recommend, is a solution of hydrochloric acid (muratic) diluted in water in a ratio of 1 part acid to 10 parts water. You can buy this by the gallon or by the quart depending on how much you need. Usually it takes about 3 gallons to wash down the average brick house.

The two most common errors committed when cleaning brickwork are using a cleaning agent that is mixed too strong, resulting in burning the joints, and not prewetting or rinsing the brick wall thoroughly to remove all of the cleaning solution.

Tools and equipment. You'll need a length of garden hose with a spray nozzle and a plastic or rubber bucket for the cleaning solution. Don't use

1. Put about 4″ of water into a plastic or rubber bucket. Wear safety goggles.

2. Pour the acid into the water, being careful not to splash it. Mix only enough to fill one-half of a 5-gallon bucket—a full bucket is too difficult to move around without spilling. If you should get the solution on your hands or in your eyes, flush with plenty of clean water. This acid is not extremely dangerous, but can burn if not removed immediately.

metal buckets, as they will react to the cleaner and could cause rust spots on the wall. A stiff bristle brush, such as those used on the farm around dairy houses, works well, and it should have a long handle to keep your hands out of the solution. A couple of broken sections of brick (half a brick or a 2″ piece) will be needed to rub stubborn spots on the wall. Don't use metal scrapers on the wall!

The accompanying photo sequence shows the correct procedure for cleaning a brick wall.

A few cleaning tips. These pointers will help your work go a lot more smoothly:

- Clean only a small area at a time so the acid solution does not dry in the brickwork and leave a stain.
- As soon as the solution gets reddish with dirt, discard it and mix fresh to prevent any staining of the wall.
- If any of the solution does get into your eyes, flush immediately with plenty of running water. If the eyes are still irritated, see a physician.

3. Spray the wall with water, making sure it's good and wet before applying any solution. Start at the top and work your way down.

4. With a long-handle brush, scrub the wall thoroughly with the acid solution, to remove all particles of mortar or dirt. Stay away from the wall as much as possible to avoid splashing your clothes.

5. To remove stubborn stains or chunks of mortar, apply an extra brushing of acid solution and rub with a piece of brick. Then scrub the spot again to remove all of the stain.

6. Rinse the wall thoroughly from top to bottom until the water runs clean.

- Never use metal scrapers on a wall—they may leave metal rust spots in the face of the brick.
- Don't pour the used acid solution near any flowers or shrubbery.
- Keep children away from the area being washed down.
- If the wind is blowing be careful that the solution does not blow back on you or on objects that could be ruined—such as the family car!
- If you have any doubt about cleaning the bricks, test a small area before tackling the entire wall.
- Don't let the solution soak into the wall for an extended period of time before flushing it down with the hose and water.
- Always read the label on the cleaner before mixing and attempting to use it.
- Store unused acid or cleaner in a safe place away from children or pets.

Cleaning the brickwork is the finishing touch to your masonry job and it is not so dangerous or hard to do. Just be careful when using the cleaner, and follow the recommended procedures and tips.

17 | Laying Stone in Mortar

Stone masonry is the art of cutting and laying stone dry or in mortar. The bonding of the stones in the wall, along with the finish of the joints, make a beautiful and rustic natural masonry wall.

Stones are one of the most overlooked building materials. They are durable, extremely attractive, and usually just lying around for the taking. They are also easy to work with since they allow a lot of room for error. A stone wall does not have to be perfectly level or plumb as brick does. Stone is laid more or less from bump to bump, but the overall alignment is plumb and level.

Working with stone can be very satisfying. The prime requirements are plenty of time to lay the stones, good mortar, determination, and a sense of design that blends the stonework with its surroundings. Most of the stonework you will do will not require a lot of cutting or complicated bond arrangements. Jobs such as sufficient retaining walls, steps, flower beds, and garden walls can be completed successfully simply by studying the information in this chapter.

You should be very careful when handling or lifting stones; it's easy to pull back muscles or suffer a nasty cut from a sharp edge. Lift with your legs, not your back. Roll a heavy stone to the wall and up a board, if need be, rather than trying to lift it onto the wall. I strongly recommend wearing a pair of safety goggles or shatterproof glasses when cutting stones because the chips really fly. Good-quality, heavy-duty work gloves for handling the stones are also a must. Leather-palm gloves work well and are fairly inexpensive.

WHERE TO FIND BUILDING STONES. The type of stonework you choose will usually indicate where to look for the stones. If you are building a rustic stone wall, for instance, try checking with a local farmer. Farmers often pick up stones in their fields and throw them in a pile somewhere on their property. As a rule, they are glad to get rid of them.

The foundations and walls of old barns are a good source of stones.

Quarried buildings stones have square edges; they need only to be cut to size.

Many old barns that are falling down generally have foundations and walls built of stones. This is a real bargain: all you have to do is get permission to back your truck up to the barn and load up the stones. The farmer may ask a nominal price, or perhaps you can give him a hand with some work around the place as an exchange.

Stones can also be found along stream banks, in old, deserted quarries that have never been cleaned out, or in old houses that have fallen in ruins. It will take some scouting around, but stones are available for the person who is willing to take the time to look for them.

You can also buy stones from a building-supply dealer. They are less rustic and usually expensive. These stones are naturally squared on the edges since they cut them for length. Make sure they are alternated in the wall to form a bond. Quarried building stones are sold by weight, with a square foot of stones figured as a certain measurement of weight. This will vary, of course, with the type of stones being sold.

If you are going to buy stones, measure the length, width, and height of the project before going to the building-supply house. Give this figure to the salesperson, who will be able to tell you approximately how many stones you need. Since quarried stones have a squared face, there is hardly any waste when laying them in the wall.

A big expense is hauling the stones to your job. As a rule, they should be put on wood pallets and set on the truck with a fork lift.

TYPES OF STONE MASONRY. The two main types of stone masonry are rubble and ashlar.

Rubble. There are two basic types of rubblestone masonry: rough and squared. Rough rubble consists of stones that are of various shapes, with rounded or angular edges. They are laid as they are picked up, and mortar is filled in between them for a natural or rustic look. Squared rubble is roughly squared or cut on the edges with a chisel and hammer. The mortar

Rough rubblestone, laid in a random pattern, makes a very pleasing wall.

Squared rubblestone lends a formal appearance to a wall. This one surrounds a swimming pool.

Example of ashlar stonework. Note that all bed and head joints are about the same width—typical of this type of masonry.

joints vary in size, however. The tops of the stones are laid somewhat level even though they are not laid in level courses. There is no special bond pattern for the wall; each stone interlocks over the one beneath it with no vertical head joints in line.

Ashlar.   In ashlar stone masonry, the stones are cut square, usually at the quarry or on the job by trained stone masons. The face of the wall will be more or less straight with a minimum of roughness in the stone surface, and all the mortar joints will be about the same thickness. This is the type of stonework found in many fine churches and educational institutions, but it is not the type the handyman would usually attempt.

TOOLS.   The regular tools you have been using for laying brick will serve most of your needs for stonework. You will also need some good chisels, a heavy-duty mash hammer, and a sledgehammer for breaking large rocks.

There are two basic chisels that come in handy for stonework: a heavy-duty pitching chisel and a point chisel (made in the shape of a point on the end). The pitching chisel is used for cutting and dressing the edges of the stones. The point chisel is used to cut off knobs on the face of the stones. A stone chisel is a lot sturdier than one used for brick. A chisel for brickwork will work out in a pinch, but if you plan to do a lot of stonework, it's better to use a stone chisel.

You'll also need a brick hammer for light shaping and cutting, a flat slicker point tool, and a rounded-off short length of broom handle for raking out the mortar joints.

MORTAR MIX.   I've found that portland cement, lime and sand make the best all-around mortar. A good mix—my favorite for stone mortar—is the type-N designation I've mentioned before: 1 part portland cement, 1 part hydrated lime, and 6 parts sand, with enough water to make it

Assortment of tools you'll need for stonework include pitching chisels and point chisel, shown at center.

Utility mixer saves work when making large quantities of mortar needed for stonework.

workable. Stone mortar should not be as soft or thin as brick mortar because it must support a greater weight. If you need a richer mix to withstand severe frost or moisture, use 1 part portland cement, ½ part hydrated lime, and 3 parts sand.

Laying stones requires a lot of mortar because you have to fill in between the irregularities in the stones. A drum-type utility mixer will save a lot of hard work mixing with a hoe. If you don't own one, it's worth borrowing one.

LAYING STONES IN MORTAR. The base of the stone wall should be laid below the frost line to prevent movement of the wall. If some big flat stones are readily available, you can lay them instead of pouring a concrete footing. This was a common practice in building stone barns and houses years ago.

To be sure of obtaining a good bond, scrape off any dirt or vegetation on the bottom of each stone before laying it in mortar. A stone should be laid on its broadest edge for the most stability. It's not a good practice to drive a lot of wedges or scraps of smaller stones beneath it to prop it up. This is necessary to a limited degree but seldom is a stone laid solidly when a lot of chips are forced under it.

The easiest method of laying out a stone wall is to build up the two ends slightly about ground level and attach a line. Then fill in with stones of various shapes and sizes. The stonework does not have to be perfectly in line with the cord—it is simply a guide.

Always try to work the bigger stones in the lower sections of a stone wall and fit smaller ones around them. The larger stones are more stable there, and it will be a lot easier on you since the heavier stones will not have to be lifted onto the wall. The best method I have found is to lay a course of stones completely across the wall without any mortar and dry-fit them first. When the arrangement satisfies you, then spread the mortar and lay them to the line in position. Minor chipping or cutting should be done before laying them in the wall.

After laying base of large stones (or concrete), build up both ends of wall above grade and attach a line. Then drybond the first course for fit.

Cutting stones.   Some stones will have to be cut or trimmed to fit in the wall. Start by laying the stone to be cut on either a piece of wood, a soft mound of earth, or the edge of the sand pile. Never lay it on a concrete floor—the shock of hitting it with a hammer or chisel may cause it to crack in the wrong place. A bench made out of old lumber works well and takes the strain out of bending over while cutting. Don't forget: wear goggles and gloves.

Mark where you want to cut with a pencil or crayon. Make sure the stone is lying solidly on the bench and will not rock or move while cutting. Slip a small wedge under the edge if necessary.

Score along the line to be cut with the chisel. Then strike a sharp blow with the hammer where you want the stone to break. With any luck it should cut evenly. If not, trim it off the best you can.

To remove any knobs or bumps on the face of the stone, use the point chisel. Rest the point of the chisel on the center of the bump and strike with the hammer. The force of the blow is concentrated in a very small area and should remove the bump. It will not crack the face of the stone if done correctly.

When cutting stone to fit, lay it on a wood platform (or a mound of earth or sand). Be sure to wear safety goggles. Here the author uses a pitching chisel to trim a stone.

Remove bumps on face of stone with a point chisel. Rest point of chisel on bump and strike with hammer.

To split a stone, lay it on the bench with grain side up. Score the entire length with chisel; then place chisel in center of stone and strike a hard blow with hammer.

If you want to split a stone that has layers, or grain, in it, prop the stone up on the bench with the grain side up. You can see this by examining the stone by eye. Cut along the grain with the chisel, scoring the entire length of the stone. When it is completely scored, strike a hard blow in the center of the grain. The stone should split, provided it is composed of layers. You will need split stones for the cap on top of the wall.

Laying the stones.   Start by dry-fitting each stone in the wall to best take advantage of its shape and size. Try not to lay the stones so vertical joints are in line; alternate stones so they break in different patterns over one another.

Lift a stone from its dry-fitted position and spread a good bed of mortar on the wall. Smear some mortar against the stone already in place to form

Dry-fit the stones into the wall, matching their contours with those already in place.

Smear a thick bed of mortar on the wall to form the bed joint, as well as against the adjacent stone to form a head joint.

Lay the stone in the mortar bed and tap it firmly with a hammer. The stone should be so solidly imbedded in the mortar that it won't rock.

Press the mortar into the joint with a pointing trowel. You can work on the head joint from front and back.

Fill gaps between the larger stones with small stones. Sighting from above, align all stones with the line.

a head joint. Lay the stone in the mortar bed and tap firmly with a hammer to make sure it is solidly placed and won't rock in the joint. Watch your fingers—the mash hammer is heavy and could injure you. With the pointing trowel, press the mortar well into the joint and around the stone. If necessary, point up the head joint front and back.

Fill in around larger stones with smaller ones where possible. (Once the bigger stones are laid, you'll find a lot of smaller ones lying around.) Fill in around each stone fully with mortar, using the trowel. Lay the stones to align as closely as possible with the nylon line you have stretched across the wall.

Finishing mortar joints. This treatment really sets off the work and makes it attractive. There are a variety of finishes you can give the mortar

One way to finish joint is to fill with a flat slicker tool . . .

. . . and then, after the mortar has set, rub with the end of a broom handle. Depth of joint is a matter of personal taste.

joints, depending on what texture or effect you want. Regardless of the finish you select, make sure that all of the mortar joints are filled, with no holes left.

One of my favorite finishes for a random rubble wall is to fill in the joint smoothly with the flat slicker tool, letting the edges protrude slightly. After the mortar has set a little, take a short length of old broom or shovel handle that has a rounded end and rub the joint slightly. (There is no specific depth—you decide how much of the stones' edges you want to show.) This gives the wall an appearance of depth and creates a nice shadow effect when the sun shines on it. After the rubbed joint has dried so it will not smear or pull away from the edge of the stone, brush with a medium-soft brush. This will close any holes or small hairline cracks in the mortar.

After joint is completely dry, brush with a medium-soft brush, closing holes or small hairline cracks in mortar.

A raked joint that was smoothed with a slicker pointing tool.

If you prefer a depressed joint that has a neater look but will still show the edges, try raking out the mortar joint with the end of the slicker tool and then point it with a flat jointer. Brush again after it has set up enough so it will not smear.

A striking tool called a concave jointer leaves a beaded joint on the surface of the mortar. The nice part about this is that the larger joints between the stones do not appear so big because the jointing tool makes all the bead joints the same size. Ask your local masonry-tool supplier for one of these if you want this finish.

Finish the wall with stones of a size to hit a level line marking the top. Make sure that top mortar joints are well filled so no water can enter the wall.

Concave jointing tool is used to form a projected bead joint.

Example of a convex bead joint in a stone wall.

FLAGSTONES. These can be bought from your local building-supply dealer in irregular or squared shapes. They are sold by weight per square foot of stone. To cut flagstone, mark where it is to be cut with a pencil and lay the stone over a piece of pipe or board, in line with the mark. With a chisel cut along the line, and the stone should break correctly.

Fit the stone in a solid bed of mortar and tap down firmly with the hammer handle. On the top of the flagstone porch shown here the stones were fitted in against the stone border and then the mortar pointed with a flat jointer. Flagstone makes very attractive walks, porches, and hearths.

To cut flagstone, lay the stone on a length of pipe, as shown, and score along the cutting line. The stone should break on the line.

Laying flagstones on the platform of a brick porch.

18 | Stone Drywalls

Stone drywalls have been popular since ancient times. Today they serve such useful and decorative purposes around the home as retaining walls or borders for flower beds, walks, and garden pathways.

"Drywall" means that no mortar is used in the laying of the stone. Some earth can be sifted between the stones to stabilize them, but the secret to a drywall's success is that the moisture can seep through without disturbing the wall since the joints are all open. Planning and building a stone drywall calls for a lot of originality. Walls can be straight or they can bend or curve however you desire.

BUILDING A DRYWALL. As a rule, no footing is needed for a drywall. The ground is excavated just a little to form a solid bed. This may be as little as 4". Since no mortar is used, freezing or frost present no problem. Tamp the earth firmly in the area where the wall is to be built to make a bed that will not rock when you lay the stones on it. You may want to spread a layer of stone screenings or even some fine crushed stone and sand to form the base; however, the stones can be laid on the bare earth with no problem.

After the first course is laid out, it's a good idea to build up the corners, then attach a line as a guide for building the wall. Lay the larger stones on the bottom section of the wall. Fit them firmly over one another so they do not wobble. It may be necessary to fit smaller pieces here and there to make the wall steady and solid. You can leave small pockets in which you can plant creeping vines or ivy.

For a stone drywall to stay in position, it should be built according to some basic rules. A drywall should be wider at its bottom and tapered on each side toward the top. This slant acts as a wedge to resist the movement of the stones in the wall. Chip stones here and there to make them fit, but don't do any extensive cutting. A handy guideline: taper a drywall about 2" for every vertical foot. The top of the wall should be one-fifth the

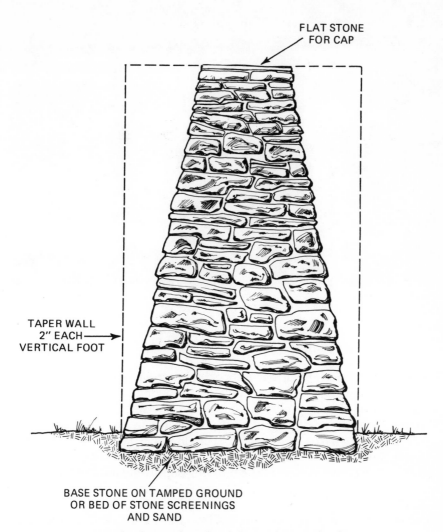

FLAT STONE FOR CAP

TAPER WALL 2″ EACH VERTICAL FOOT

BASE STONE ON TAMPED GROUND OR BED OF STONE SCREENINGS AND SAND

Example of stone drywall with battered (tapered) sides.

thickness of the bottom. If the stones have flat edges, such as fieldstones do, the slant can be as little as 1″ to the foot. If a wall is built of rounded stones, it may be necessary to taper it 3″ to the foot.

Don't lay stones like bricks—in courses. The stones near the top of the wall should be lighter in weight. Fill in with soil to hold them in place. The key to building a good drywall is to make sure each stone is supporting itself. The stones must bond, or interlock, with ones below it. Bond stones also should be laid which extend from the front to the back of the wall. They don't have to fit perfectly but should be somewhere close to the wall's width.

This type of bond is called rubble stonework, and anyone can do it with some determination and patience. Let some of the stones jut out of the wall to form brackets for plants or to break up the outline.

Stone drywall built to retain earth between two different grades.

A curved wall is stronger than a straight one and is particularly effective for a retaining wall to build up an existing grade. Use a garden hose as a guide in laying the first course.

Excessive water buildup against a drywall can ruin it. If the wall is at the bottom of a hill where there is a lot of runoff, it may be wise to dig a small gutter to divert the water along the wall. If a severe water problem exists, pick up a few drainage tiles at the building-supply dealer and build them into the wall at approximately grade line. They will help to relieve water buildup.

For the ends and corners of the wall, you will have to be a little more fussy in selecting stones; the corners should be somewhat straight without too many projecting knobs or edges. Also, build in plenty of bond stones to tie the wall at these points. If a gate or frame is to be attached to the wall, the same procedure should be followed, as this will be a weak point. Remember, building a good drywall is harder than laying stone mortar since there is nothing to hold the stones in place but the weight and interlocking of one stone against the other. It is amazing, however, how strong a properly built drywall can be, and you don't need any masonry experience to build one.

DRYWALL CREATIVITY. A drywall makes an attractive backdrop and retaining wall for a pool on the side of a hill. You will have to pack earth or mud around the stones in the bottom of the pool to prevent the water from leaking through, or put concrete in the bottom of the pool area. If there is runoff from a nearby stream, this makes a perfect setup: the water

Stone drywall built to form a pool and waterfall.

Stone pier laid in mortar backed up with a drywall. Top of pier is built in form of a lantern with kerosene torch and wick in base.

Stone drywall with concrete cap.

Unusual stone pyramid and rounded pier built of dry stone.

can be run through a pipe in the stone wall or diverted to the pool area. A few goldfish in the pool add more beauty to the project and will also help eliminate insects on the surface of the water.

Drywalls, in combination with stone walls laid in mortar, create striking additions to a garden. The stone pier topped with a Japanese lantern design and butted with a drywall, for example, highlight this walk. The steps are railroad ties laid with steel pegs to hold them in position. Gravel forms the treads of the steps. The block wall to the right will be veneered with fieldstone later to finish the job.

Drywalls can be built with a concrete cap poured on top of the wall to hold it in place. This used to be done around a lot of old graveyards years ago. Many of them are still standing and in good condition.

19 | Restoring an Old Stone Fireplace

Many fireplaces found in old homes can be restored and made safe to burn again if the chimney is in good shape and still solid. The trend to restore masonry work rather than demolish it and build new is based on sound reasoning, provided the deterioration has not gone too far. Many of these old fireplaces have historical value and should be preserved.

The stone fireplace shown in this chapter is a good example of what a handyman can do—with a minimum of expense. This is the kind of project that can be worked on a little at a time, with a great deal of tender loving care. All you have to do is buy mortar and a damper, and round up some stones. You don't have to be an expert stone mason; the work is not that difficult. The job is time-consuming, but the end result will be well worth the effort.

INSPECT AND TEST THE CHIMNEY. Before starting any fireplace repair work, you have to find out if the chimney and fireplace are safe to use. The easiest inspection is to look up the chimney through the firebox using a strong flashlight. You can generally tell if the brick lining is bad or burnt out. Don't be alarmed if you can't see daylight all the way up the chimney. Many old chimneys were built on an incline so they would work out next to the center of the roof ridge board. Just be concerned with the condition of the masonry work. For another view, get up on the roof with a mirror that reflects the sunlight down the chimney, or use a strong flashlight, and look at the condition of the brickwork.

If you'd feel better if a professional looked the job over, contact a masonry contractor. In many areas fire departments will conduct chimney inspections for a donation. If the repair work is going to be extensive—cutting out the front of the chimney from top to bottom and inserting new flue linings, for instance—leave the job to a professional mason.

If there is more than one flue in the chimney, you may want to make a smoke test to discover possible leaks between flues. To do this, build a

Stone fireplace before work was begun.

smudge fire at the bottom of the flue and, while the smoke is flowing freely, cover the top of the chimney tightly. Smoke escaping into other flues or through mortar joints indicates openings that must be repointed with mortar or bricks that must be replaced. Open some doors or windows in the house to allow the smoke to clear. You will, of course, have to be very careful if making a test in a house that is occupied or has furniture stored in it. It's a good idea to warn the neighbors, too; you don't want the fire department out on a false alarm.

REJUVENATING THE FIREPLACE.　The fireplace shown in this chapter did not require extensive work. On inspection, the flue area was found to be in good condition. For many years the firebox opening had been closed off and a wood stove connected to the fireplace flue to heat the home. A thorough examination showed the old fireplace would be as good as new, even better, with these additions: a new firebox; a damper installed with a smoke shelf; the stone jambs extended to form a 42″ opening; the stone face of the fireplace repointed with new mortar; and a raised outer hearth.

The first job was to tear out the old brick firebox, which was soft and had deteriorated from fires of many years past. A new firebox of firebrick would have to be built to replace it.

My friend, for whom I was doing the job, knew that the house was very old, but not exactly how old. When we removed the back of the firebox, we discovered a metal plate attached to the back wall. Its purpose was to reflect the heat of the fire into the room. After cleaning it off with a brush,

Old cast-iron plate found in back of fireplace with German inscriptions.

we found the plate was cast iron with an inscription in German. Close examination unearthed a date: *1742.* This was an unexpected find. The old cast-iron plate now resides in the room next to the fireplace as a conversation piece, and its owner is very proud of it. The figures and inscription, we feel sure, inspire good luck; it was the custom in many of the early homes in this area to have such a talisman.

As we removed the old brick, we also discovered that the lintel, which supported the brickwork over the opening, was laid on an old metal wagon

Stone fireplace with old brick firebox removed. This is the original fireplace as it was built. The blackened area in the back is evidence that fireplace was used before brick firebox was added.

New brick firebox was installed and stonework built up to the wood lintel.

spoke, another of my friend's treasures, along with the metal plate. Many old handmade nails rounded out the assortment of items we found while tearing out the firebox. When the back of the stone chimney was exposed, we could see where the original fires had burned before the brick firebox was built. The stonework was in good shape, but it needed repointing.

We wanted a finished fireplace opening 42″ wide. This meant building in the stonework on each side to that size. There were still a lot of stones lying around the property, so it was no problem to round up enough and lay them in mortar to form the opening. A good mortar recommendation for stonework is 1 part portland cement, 1 part lime, and 6 parts sand.

The firebrick hearth was laid first, followed by the stonework up to the height of the lintel. Then firebrick was laid on the sides and in the back and filled in behind the mortar and small stones.

We installed a rotary-control damper in a bed of mortar on top of the brick firebox approximately 7″ higher than the top of the opening. The area in back of the firebox was leveled off even with the bottom of the damper to form a smoke shelf. We set the steel angle iron over the opening and laid the stonework across it, sealing it off against the wood beam.

Repointing the stonework. The mortar joints in the stonework were in bad condition and had to be repointed with new mortar. The first step was to cut out the old and defective mortar to an approximate depth of ¾″. This was done with a plugging chisel.

Cutting out old mortar joints with a plugging chisel to a depth of ¾ ".

Wetting the cut-out joint with a brush and water.

As we removed all of the loose mortar, we brushed out the joint and wet it with water, using an old paintbrush. Don't saturate the joint with water, merely dampen it. This slows down the set of the pointing mortar and lets it cure properly.

To prepare the pointing mortar, mix in the proportions previously described, using only enough water to be able to press the mix into a damp ball. After letting it set for approximately one-half hour, add more water to make it workable for pointing. Called prehydrating the mortar, this helps to cut down on the shrinkage that takes place. A flat jointing tool

Repointing the mortar in joint with a flat slicker tool.

Raking out the mortar joint with a rounded-off length of broom handle.

Cleaning off the old lime from the stone with a wire brush.

called a slicker is used to compress the mortar well into the joint. If the joints are especially wide, a small pointing trowel comes in handy.

After repointing the mortar, you can finish the joints several ways: flat and smooth, raked out, or simply brushed (wait until they have cured enough so they won't smear). On this particular job, I used a short length of an old rounded broom handle to rake out the joints slightly. This allowed the edges to show a little more and created a nice depth effect. After the joint had set a little, I brushed it off to complete the repointing process.

Over the years lime paint and other substances had been applied to the face of the stonework. A wire brush did a good job of removing the old paint and other materials from the surface. It's important, though, not to work the brush across the newly pointed joints any more than is necessary until they have cured.

Finishing the fireplace. When we finished repointing, we built the outer hearth of stones recovered from the property. (If there is an old stone fence around, it will serve as a good source of stones.) Flat stones were picked for the hearth surface. They were cleaned off with a stiff brush to remove any dirt or smears.

The old beam which ran across the center of the fireplace wall had dried out from years of being inside the house. A coating of linseed oil rubbed into the wood helped to restore its natural beauty. A firescreen or glass fire doors were to be added later to finish the job.

The restored fireplace ready for use.

20 | More Masonry Projects

BRICK BARBECUE. This project will require approximately 250 bricks. (Buy about 25 extra to allow for damage during delivery.) Select hard bricks that will withstand the weather. Since the top course is a header, you want bricks without holes in them. If you think some brick paving would be nice in front of the barbecue later, now is the time to buy those bricks. Even though all bricks in one color range are supposed to be the same, variances in burning will make a noticeable difference.

Building the foundation. Since the project is not too large, the most practical way to install the footing is to excavate the entire area and pour 6″ of concrete to serve as a pad. Lay some reinforcement, such as pieces of old fence, metal scraps, pipe, or some concrete reinforcement wire for extra strength. Use a mix of 1 part portland cement, 2 parts sand, and 3 parts stone. A utility mixer, if you have access to one, will make mixing the concrete easier than mixing with a hoe in a wheelbarrow. Make sure that the wire or other reinforcement is well imbedded in the concrete when it is poured.

The foundation can be built of old bricks or concrete bricks—whichever you already have or can buy cheaply. Remember, this work will not be seen; it is only to support the barbecue below the grade line. Fill in the center of the foundation, level with the top of the foundation walls, with scraps of old block.

Pouring the concrete slab. At the finished grade line, form and pour a concrete slab 4″ thick on the foundation. Lay some metal reinforcement in the concrete again for extra strength. The slab will support the brick walls of the barbecue, and the center will serve as the hearth or bottom of the firebox, which is used when cooking with wood.

Building the brick walls. Lay up the double brick wall as shown in the plan. Be sure to keep it as wide as the header bricks that will be used at

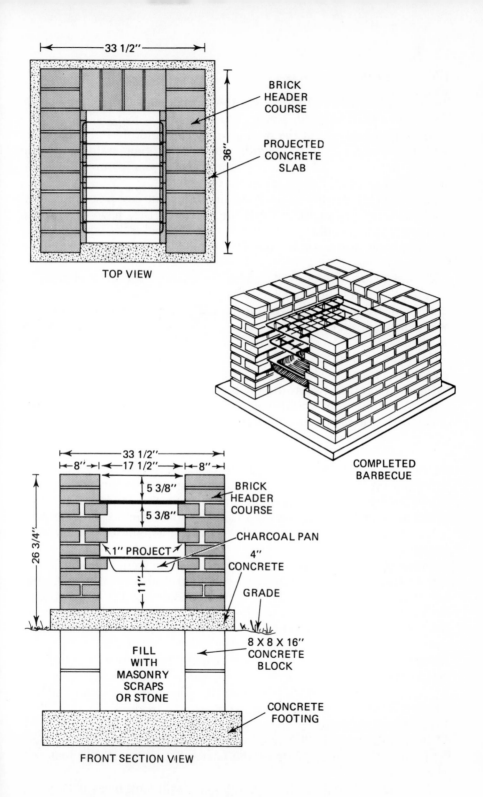

TOP VIEW

33 1/2''

36''

BRICK
HEADER
COURSE

PROJECTED
CONCRETE
SLAB

COMPLETED
BARBECUE

FRONT SECTION VIEW

33 1/2''

8'' 17 1/2'' 8''

5 3/8''

5 3/8''

26 3/4''

1'' PROJECT

11''

BRICK
HEADER
COURSE

CHARCOAL PAN

4''
CONCRETE

GRADE

8 X 8 X 16''
CONCRETE
BLOCK

FILL
WITH
MASONRY
SCRAPS
OR STONE

CONCRETE
FOOTING

175

the top of the wall to cap it off. On the fourth course, project the inside bricks about 1″ on both side walls. They will hold the charcoal pan. On the sixth course again set out the brickwork on the inside 1″ to hold a grate. Set out the bricks 1″ in the eighth course for another grate. The three set-outs on the inside of the barbecue wall enable you to move the grates or charcoal pan to different levels for cooking.

You can get grates from a local welding shop. The cast-iron grates used in old floor-furnace registers work fine, too, after they have been cut to size. Stay away from old refrigerator or metal-coated racks, however; they may have zinc or lead on them, which could be poisonous if absorbed in food.

The last course of bricks will be a header course. It serves two functions: (1) it ties the double brick wall together, and (2) it forms a cap to finish the job. A concave joint works well on the walls. The top mortar head joints between the headers should be struck with a flat tool so water does not lie in the joints.

Use a mason's rule to keep the work on correct course height, and make sure the walls are level all the way around the project. Don't fill in with too much mortar between the double walls; this tends to push out the work. When the brickwork is completed, brush it off with a wire brush.

This barbecue can be used with either charcoal or wood, with the grates adjusted for the flame.

OUTDOOR STONE FIREPLACE. A rubblestone fireplace gives you an opportunity to express yourself in stone. Start once again with a good foundation built below the frost line in your area. You can install a footing or pad as in the barbecue and lay a block foundation up to grade, or pour concrete in the excavated area, along with some chunks of rock lying around to form the foundation.

Gather up some stones from around the place (or from a nearby farmer with a pile or old tumbledown fence). Any kind of stones will do, but avoid large ones—they'll require a lot of cutting. Build up the stonework as shown, and make the hearth of stone, also. Use masonry-cement mortar or a mixture of 1 part portland cement, 1 part hydrated lime, and 6 parts sand.

The top of the side walls, at the point where the stonework sets back for the chimney, should be fairly level to support utensils when cooking. The side walls are approximately 4″ higher than the grate to permit building the grate into the stonework. You can have a grate made at a welding shop, or use short lengths of ½″ to ⅝″ steel reinforcement rods.

The hearth can be built of flagstones, if you don't want to use firebrick. Point all of the mortar joints on the hearth flat with a slicker tool or a pointing trowel.

The front and back walls of the chimney will look nicer if they are slightly tapered toward the top. From the set-back area above the grille

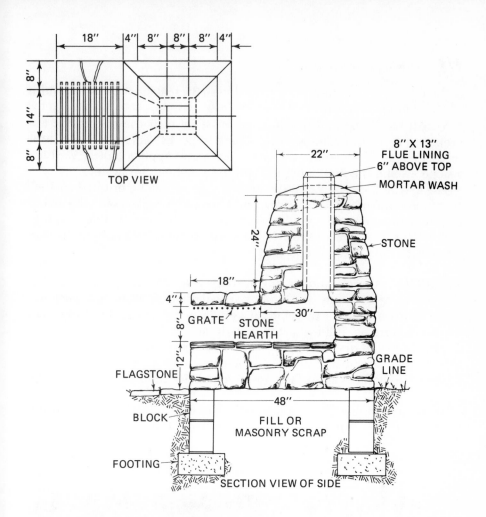

18" 4" 8" 8" 8" 4"

8"

14"

8"

TOP VIEW

22"

8" X 13"
FLUE LINING
6" ABOVE TOP

MORTAR WASH

24"

STONE

18"

4"

GRATE

30"

STONE
HEARTH

8"

12"

FLAGSTONE

GRADE
LINE

BLOCK

48"

FILL OR
MASONRY SCRAP

FOOTING

SECTION VIEW OF SIDE

FINISHED
FIREPLACE

to the top of the chimney, draw in each wall 3″, making it 24″—the width of the chimney—at the top.

A steel bar or angle iron will have to be set over the opening of the firebox to carry the chimney wall. Use a 9″ × 13″ flue lining and let it project about 6″ above the top of the chimney. Apply a mortar wash on a slope around the flue lining at the top to seal out any water.

The mortar joints between the fireplace stones can be brushed and left as they are, smoothed with a trowel and brushed, or raked out with an old length of broom handle and brushed. They should look a little rough to match the stone. As a finishing touch, you can lay some flagstones in sand around the completed fireplace.

SANDBOX A brick sandbox in your back yard will give your children a clean place to have fun, and is not particularly difficult to construct.

Dig an excavation for the sandbox as indicated in the sketch and install the wooden frame. Fill the sandbox with sand and surround with a 1×4 edging. Spread a dry mixture of 3 parts sand to 1 part cement over the ground area around the sandbox, and tamp and grade as necessary to achieve a smooth, even surface. Place solid brick units directly upon this cushion base.

Upon completion of the sandbox, sweep clean sand into cracks between the brick units. Clean with a gentle spray from the garden hose.

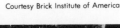

Courtesy Brick Institute of America

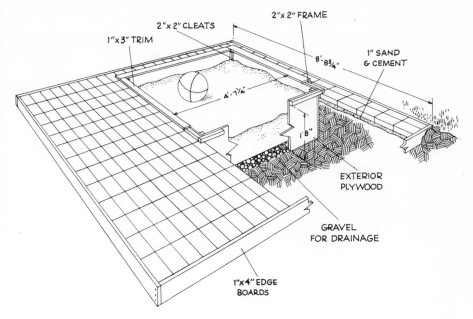

2"x 2" FRAME

2"x 2" CLEATS

1"x3" TRIM

2"x 2" FRAME

1" SAND & CEMENT

8'·8¾"

4'·7¼"

1'·8"

EXTERIOR PLYWOOD

GRAVEL FOR DRAINAGE

1"x4" EDGE BOARDS

Courtesy Brick Institute of America

Materials

    240 solid brick units 3¾" × 2¼" × 8" or 4" × 8" × 1⅝"

    about 5 cubic feet of damp, loose sand (¼ ton) (does not include sand
      for sandbox)

    1¼ cubic feet of cement or 1¼ bags of portland cement

    galvanized nails

    ⅝" exterior-grade, rough-sawn plywood siding, coated with preserva-
      tive, cut as follows:

                4 lengths of 20" × 55⅜"

                4 lengths of 2" × 2" × 7'

                4 lengths of 1" × 4" × 9'

                2 lengths of 1" × 3" × 10'

STEPPING STONES: Here's a brick project you can build in just a few
hours that will add beauty and interest to your yard for years to come.

    Stepping stones are most conveniently placed about 4" apart. For each
step, excavate a square hole 4" deep, large enough to accommodate a
17½" frame (outside dimensions) of redwood plank. Position the frame in
the excavation so that its top is level with the grass line. Mix 1 part cement
to 3 parts sand and spread 1" to 1½" of this mixture, dry, in the hole. Tamp
it down; add more if needed to bring it near the level of the frame. Lay
the brick units on the cushion in the pattern shown; make sure they are
flush with the top of the frame.

Materials

for 10 squares 16″ × 16″:

80 solid brick units 3¾″ × 2¼″ × 8″
10 lengths redwood plank 1″ × 4″ × 6″
fivepenny galvanized box nails
3 cubic feet sand (about 260 pounds)
1 bag (94 pounds) portland cement

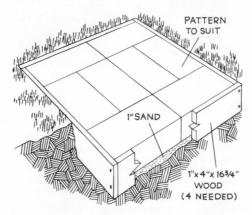

Courtesy Brick Institute of America

PEDESTAL. This brick pedestal, designed to provide a dramatic setting for your favorite flower arrangement, is so easy to build you may just want to supervise and let the children have fun creating your new garden addition.

Because no mortar is used in its construction, it is important to have a level, stable base for the pedestal. Gravel may be used, but a concrete slab is best. The slab should be 16″ × 12″ square and about 4″ thick. Make sure the footing is excavated deep enough to go below the frost line.

Place the brick as shown. As you go along, lay each course so that the brick units overlay the cracks between the units on the level below.

Materials needed: 30 bricks and ½ cubic foot of concrete (1 bag premixed concrete).

Courtesy Brick Institute of America

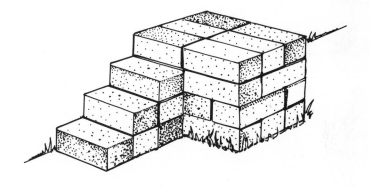

Index